Praise for

The Last Lighthouse Keeper

Stuart McDowell does a magnificent job crafting a holistic tale of light-houses—and a light keeper—along the California coast. He deftly weaves the story of light keeper Bill Owens and his family with their life at iconic coastal lighthouses.

This captivating tale is portrayed in a fascinating and engaging man-ner, thanks to McDowell's skills as a seamless storyteller. We learn of the Owens family's thirty-two years of trials, challenges, and triumphs, along with shipwrecks, lighthouse history, and the subsequent battles between civil-ian employees and their military overlords. The story was so wonderfully told that I was in tears by the end of the read.

—**Tom Wilmer,** travel journalist, producer and host of the Lowell Thomas Award-winning NPR Podcast "Journey's of Discovery with Tom Wilmer"

What makes The Last Lighthouse Keeper *soar as historical intrigue is McDowell's passion for his subject, his keen understanding of the Central California Coast, and his rare ability to make history come alive. The story is so vivid you can smell the salt air.*

—**Bob Welch,** author of *Saving My Enemy* and *The Wizard of Foz.*

The Last Lighthouse Keeper *is a book you will love. Stuart McDowell is a delightful storyteller and brings Bill and Isabel Owens to life again through his insights into their lives at four California light stations. With a deep his-torical context as background, McDowell writes of the hardships and respon-sibilities of this unique, pre-automation profession of light keeper. He does an excellent job of making this tale personal—and touching.*

—**Jean Anton,** retired educator, Board of Directors, Heritage Society of Pacific Grove

What an outstanding book! Our docents at Point Arena all have favor-ite Owens anecdotes that we have accumulated over the years, and Stuart

McDowell's thorough, entertaining, and highly personal book about Bill Owens has given us many more. McDowell delivers a rich telling of the adventures of Bill Owens—a well lived and dedicated life.

    —**Mark Hancock,** Executive Director, Point Arena Light Station

In our wildest dreams, my sisters and I never thought the Owens family would be the subject of a book. And yet, Stuart McDowell saw something in our father and was passionate about wanting to tell his story. He did so with honor for our family, respect for the nuances of Bill and Isabel Owens, and diligence for the truth. The result is a story that we are both humbled and proud to call accurate and honoring in regard to our father, right down to the way he always called the piano a "pie-anna!"

    —**Diana Owens Brown**, daughter of Bill and Isabel Owens

Also by Stuart McDowell

The Sinking of the SS Montebello

Great Tidepool Press

Pacific Grove, California

Front cover: Keeper Owens on-watch at Point Arena. (Courtesy of Point Cabrillo Light Keepers Association)

Cover design by Bob Welch

All photos in the book without credits are public-domain images.

ISBN: 9798389163799

Print No. 042523.235p

To contact the author: mcdowellsinpg@yahoo.com

The Last Lighthouse Keeper

The Seasons, Storms, and Shipwrecks
of California's Bill Owens

Stuart McDowell

Great Tidepool Press

Pacific Grove, California

I can think of no other edifice constructed by man
as altruistic as a lighthouse.
They were built only to serve.

—George Bernard Shaw

For Caren McDowell

My wife of forty-two years, who, long ago, decided that one of her life goals would be to help me achieve mine.

The Lighthouses Served by Bill Owens

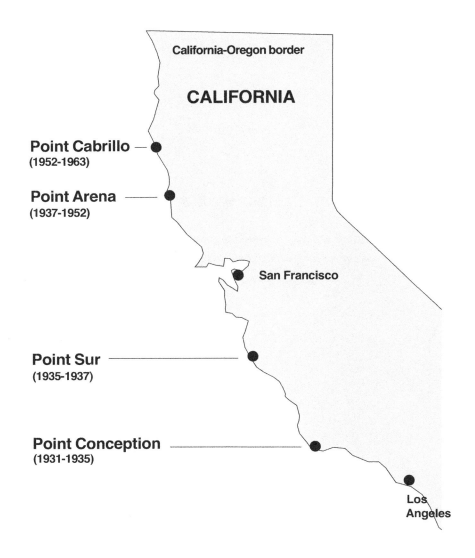

Table of Contents

Author's Note

It was summer 1982, a time when Ronald Reagan served as president, Great Britain's war with Argentina over the Falkland Islands ended, and the Equal Rights Amendment failed for lack of support.

I was twenty-eight years old, Caren twenty-five. Married only twelve months, we hopped onto the train at Union Station in Los Angeles, where our bicycles had been safely stowed. Our plan was to arrive in Eugene, Oregon, then cycle to Florence on the coast and head south along California's Coast Highway to San Francisco, a journey of more than 700 miles.

Along the way, I hoped to connect with a retired light keeper who I'd learned of while reading the book *America's Sunset Coast*. His name was Bill Owens. He lived with his wife, Isabel, on the coast just south of Mendocino, California.

Growing up on the California coast, I had visited numerous lighthouses in my early years. The allure of light stations, their keepers, and the shipwrecks beyond them had grabbed me as a young boy and never let go. If it were possible to meet face-to-face with a living lighthouse keeper, I was committed to making it happen.

I wrote a proverbial "note in a bottle" expressing my deep interest, sent it off to the couple, and quickly received a reply that nearly knocked me off my feet. "We'll expect to see you soon," Isabel had written.

Caren and I had cycled 540 miles before reaching Mendocino and the Owens home on August 2, 1982. Outside their front door, fittingly, was a ship's bell that we, of course, rang. Bill and Isabel politely invited us in.

As our interview began, I asked Bill if he was often "pestered" by lighthouse enthusiasts like me knocking on his door. "Well, let's see," he said, "there was National Geographic in '75, Ralph Shanks in '78. And, now, you."

A veiled look of disappointment shadowed his face. He told us the work of the lighthouse keeper didn't seem to matter to people anymore. It was, therefore, meaningful to him and Isabel that "two young people" were so curious about his life at the lights.

Our pre-arranged one-day visit turned into three days of fascinating interviews, even if I had no idea what I might eventually do with the information once I learned it. To me, the fascination wasn't in the translating of his life to others—I was a school psychologist—but, like a historian, in the story itself.

Their living room was warmed by a blazing wood-burning stove. Bill was perpetually cold, his daughters later told us. He sat aside the stove in perfect comfort while we peeled away sweatshirts and mopped perspiration from our brows.

From the beginning, Caren and I were captivated by the couple. They shared memories from each light station at which they'd lived: Point Conception, Point Sur, Point Arena, and finally, Point Cabrillo.

Bill told us of storms, shipwrecks, rumrunning, and duties at the light station during World War II. Of spotting a submarine in December 1941 off the light at Point Arena. He called the Navy in San Francisco, which shooshed him away like a pesky fly. "Oh, go back to bed," he was told. "We don't have any subs in that area."

Two days later, the SS *Emidio* was torpedoed by a Japanese sub off Cape Mendocino.

"Did the Navy get back to you?" I asked.

"Yep," he said. "The next day, a whole parade of naval officers come up from San Francisco to the light station and swore me to secrecy for the duration of the war. I suppose they're all admirals now."

Bill was that way. To judge by the expression on his face, he had little sense of humor. But that was hardly the case. He had a wry wit about him that surfaced frequently, a stubbornness that was more endearing than annoying, and a pride in his thirty-two years of service that was obvious. He expressed them all as he told us about earthquakes, plane crashes, dirigible disasters—and the less exciting, but more enduring, job of him and Isabel raising a family of six girls at the stations, one season of life transitioning into another.

With Bill and Isabel's permission, I tape-recorded portions of our conversations—six hour's worth. The interviews formed the foundation of an underdog's story—one you don't know but should. It is the story of a young couple in the Lighthouse Service who faced a string of obstacles—the Great Depression, two world wars, lighthouse isolation, devastating loss, and more—but, together, overcame them all.

Later, I made several return visits. On each occasion Bill and Isabel insisted I stay with them. Two years after we first met, Bill passed away at age eighty-three. Isabel stayed in touch with us for more than a decade, until her death in 1995 at the age of ninety-one. I saved all thirty of the letters she sent, each one steeped with the gentle warmth that embodied her life.

In 2021, after my book about another Japanese submarine torpedoing a U.S. civilian ship (*The Sinking of the SS* Montebello) was finished, I knew it was time to tell Bill's story. By then, it had been nearly forty years since I had first interviewed him and Isabel. I blended the information from those interviews—more than 100 transcribed pages—with remembrances from all six of their children, and made multiple visits to the light stations at Sur, Arena, and Cabrillo. (Point Conception is inaccessible due to Coast Guard restrictions. No visitors are allowed). I pored through hundreds of newspaper articles, read books, and dug up the contextual history that was coursing through the country while Bill kept watch from 1931 to 1963.

The result is the unique story of Bill Owens, the last of a generation of civilian light keepers along the California Coast before automated lighthouses rendered them unnecessary.

I am now sixty-nine years old, and so grateful that, as a twenty-eight-year-old young man, I chose to stand on the Owens porch and sound that ship's bell. I hope the story that rang forth—and that I've finally turned into a book—will enrich you as much as it has me.

Stuart McDowell
Pacific Grove, California
May 2023

United States Lighthouse Service stopwatch used to time the light and fog-signal. The date matches Bill's first year as a lighthouse keeper.

Prologue

For as long as man has gone to sea, lighted beacons have guided his ships to port. To the mariner, the lighthouse is a sentry announcing potential danger. At the same time, the beacon is a reassuring landmark of security. It is the last thing ashore a ship's crew sees when sailing for open ocean—and the first thing they see upon return.

By 1949, the Point Arena Lighthouse had already been luminating this stretch of the Northern California coast for seventy-nine years. The point, just north of town, is the first promontory of significance north of Point Reyes—the closest point of land in the continental U.S. to Hawaii. And it had seen its share of shipwrecks over the centuries. The most recent had been the *Dorothy Wintermote* in 1938, just after Keeper Bill Owens had transferred to Point Arena from the Point Sur Light Station in Big Sur.

The *Wintermote* was referred to as a "tramp freighter" and hauled basic goods and lumber up and down the North Coast. The ship was steaming from San Francisco to Portland when, in a dense fog, she ran aground on rocks just south of Point Arena. The crew of twenty-nine was saved but the ship sank three days later—a total loss.

Another hazard, Arena Rock, lies just beneath the water line and barely a mile northwest of the point. Referred to as "Wash Rock" by the local populous, the dangerous outcropping has thirteen feet of water over it at mean tide. The shipmaster's guidebook, the *Pacific Coast Pilot*, states the rock shows "a breaker except in very smooth weather … it should be given a good berth as it rises abruptly from deep water." Arena Rock seems small near the surface. But below the water line, the rock covers an area the size of a football field.

In a way, Bill Owens had something in common with Arena Rock: there was more to him than appeared on the surface. Physically, he was a small man, but he had a commanding—almost intimidating—presence. Bill tended to speak in short, and sometimes blunt, sentences but he loved engaging in conversation with others. He had little formal education but possessed a sharp and retentive mind. And though, as an orphaned child, he had lived in poverty and uncertainty, Bill became a dependable provider for his family, like a lighthouse, a fixture one could count on.

And much like Arena Rock, it would be easy to underestimate him.

The summer of 1949 had been a pleasant time at the light station. With the longer days—sunlight was still present at 9 P.M.—the evening watch duties seemed shorter. And there were rarely any storms. The sound of laughter sprinkled the station, coming from his children who now played across the lighthouse property, or "reservation."

On Saturdays, visitors flocked to the station for tours of the light tower and fog-signal building. On clear afternoons, the California sun immersed everything in a golden shimmer. Summer had its own wonderful pace and appearance.

There was, of course, plenty of coastal fog, especially prevalent during the summer months. It was always a concern to keepers. Fog could sweep in quickly off the horizon, cloaking ships in a hazardous grey shroud. For the mariner's safety, the keeper's watch-duty included being alert to changes in weather conditions, especially waves of fog approaching. In such circumstances, the fog-signal would be immediately activated. But it wasn't like the old days when the steam powered fog-whistle required keepers to burn two-thirds of a cord of wood to produce ten hours of steam. Air compressors and generators now powered the signal-blast with the flick of a switch.

A few years before, Owens had been promoted to officer-in-charge at Point Arena. He, Isabel, and their children had been transferred here in 1937. During the dozen years since, the Owens family had become part of the Point Arena fabric, their lives interwoven with the town, the people, and particularly the light station.

It was a life that fit them to near-perfection. Bill loved the work and the importance of it. Isabel had grown up on a Maryland farm and loved what she referred to as the "wide open spaces." Here, she had such views in abundance. The couple would ultimately have six daughters who all grew to adulthood on light stations. Each of them lived a unique childhood filled with the freedom, adventure, responsibility, and independence that life on a lighthouse offered—and all to a degree their childhood peers could hardly imagine.

Nearly all the school-aged years of the Owens children had been lived right here. Holidays, birthdays, summer vacations, and family events had taken place on the light station. Their sixth child, Diana, had been born on the station. And for the Owens girls, every day offered adventures on, and around, the beaches, tidepools, and fields of the lighthouse property.

Point Arena was home.

Bill was now in his eighteenth year with the United States Lighthouse Service. The USLHS had been absorbed by the Coast Guard in a cost-saving move by the Roosevelt administration in 1939. Thus, technically, Bill was a civil servant under the auspices of the Coast Guard.

It was a vocation that almost did not avail itself to Bill Owens.

In 1931, the Great Depression, like a tidal wave, was drowning Americans in joblessness, hunger, and economic misery. Bill was one of the lucky ones. He had employment at the Bethlehem Shipyards in San Francisco. On weekends, he enjoyed pursuing one of the great loves of his life—fishing. He often packed his pole and tackle-box and rode the ferry across the bay to Angel Island. It was there, in 1930, that he had a conversation with a stranger who would change his life forever.

"He talked lighthouse employment up pretty good," Bill remembered. "A fellow by the name of Reit. From the way he talked, you got your quarters furnished and everything. It sounded like a pretty good deal, so, I put in for it."

The stranger, Carl Reit, was the head keeper at Point Knox Lighthouse on the island. A native of Norway, Reit had come to the United States as a young man and had worked in the Lighthouse Service for thirty years. As the two men fished side by side that Sunday, their conversation lit a fire in Bill. His wife later said, "That's when he decided being a lighthouse keeper was the life for him ."

The process, however, would be a hard-fought one for Owens; one that, for several months, appeared to be a lost cause.

He took the examination and made number one on the list. Captain Harry Rhodes was superintendent of the 18th District at that time.

"I'd get letters saying, 'You are one of three selected for such-and-such a station. Would you accept the position if offered?' I'd send back the response each time. 'Yes.' And I wouldn't hear anything."

Tired of the runaround, Owens marched down to the Lighthouse Services' office at Custom House on San Francisco's Battery Street. "I wanted to know why I wasn't getting any of these jobs."

Rhodes told him, "Well, we don't have quarters big enough for you and your children." At the time, Bill and Isabel had three daughters between the ages of one and four.

But Captain Rhodes, it turned out, had an additional concern. Bill Owens was small of stature. At the time he applied for the Lighthouse Service, he stood five-feet nine-inches tall and weighed only 123 pounds. The job, Rhodes knew, would require strength.

"You're too light to start the engines at this station."

"I wasn't too light when I was packing a gun all over France during the War," Bill fired back.

"You've been offered three stations," said Rhodes, obviously unmoved. "You didn't qualify for any of them. You're off the list.'"

Owens walked out of the office more angry than discouraged. And he certainly wasn't giving up. "Bill was a fighter when it was something he wanted," Isabel said. "And he wanted that job."

He knew he was small, but he was a pipefitter at Bethlehem Shipyards, a huge provider of U.S. ships; he had sturdy hands and forearms. He was wiry-strong. He knew that, if only given the chance, he could perform whatever was required of him.

When, the next day, he shared his concerns with his supervisor at Bethlehem, the man listened attentively.

"Let's go down and see my brother-in-law tonight and see what he says."

The man's brother-in-law was U.S. Congressman Richard J. Welch. At the time, 1931, he was Chairman for the Committee on Labor (and would ultimately be elected to twelve straight Congresses).

When the three met at the lawmaker's office, Welch not only listened, but asked questions. About Bill's work experience, his education, his family, and his military experience.

"Let's see what we can do," he said, drawing the meeting to an end. "I'll be in touch."

The next morning, Welch had his chauffeur drive him to the Custom House to see Captain Harry Rhodes. Rhodes paid little heed to the congressman. But Welch persisted. On June 24, he wrote a letter—on Owens' behalf—to the Acting Commissioner of Lighthouses, H.D. King, in Washington, D.C. A week later, Welch received a reply from King stating that his request was under consideration.

Twelve days later, Bill and Isabel were getting ready for bed when they heard a knock on the door. It was a telegram delivery. The message said simply: "You are hereby appointed as assistant keeper at Point Conception Light Station."

The two hugged in celebration. The next morning, Bill was to report straight to Rhodes. As he entered the superintendent's office, Bill suppressed, as best he could, his satisfaction at landing the job.

"You know, it's not a good idea to go to a congressman," said Rhodes, who'd already been told to hire Owens.

"It served me alright. I got a job."

"Well, you're going to Conception. I hope you take care of your job."

"Thank you," he said. "I intend to."

Bill was now an employee of the United States Lighthouse Service. And the word "service" meant something to Owens. The duties of the lightkeeper, he felt, were indeed a needed service to every mariner and ship at sea. The light signal provided each vessel a bearing on their location in the darkness; the fog-signal gave the same safety and protection in poor visibility. To do the job well required sacrifice, hard work, and discipline. The new keeper was adept at all three.

Bill was justifiably proud of the profession—and of the responsibilities. Each light station required keepers to work as a team, to be prepared for their watches—when the operation of the light and fog-signal had to be monitored continuously. Any malfunction could be catastrophic to a ship at sea and had to be remedied immediately. The work was tiring, demanding, and sometimes, Owens would come to learn, hazardous.

Now, in 1949, stationed at Point Arena, Owens presided over a competent and efficient light station, whose reservation was well kept. The critical navigational aids—the light beacon and fog-signal—were maintained in excellent working order. The men assigned to operate and stand watch over them were well-trained and reliable. Owens had earned a reputation of "running a good light."

Along with his pride in the efficiency of the station was his appreciation of the splendor of

Bill Owens, with his ever-present pipe, outside the lantern room atop the tower at Point Arena circa 1942. (Courtesy of Point Arena Light Keepers)

the setting itself. The lighthouse reservation at Point Arena was a picturesque sight to behold. Cows grazed in the ranch fields that bordered the ocean. Within the gate of the station, four lovely wooden cottages, each two-storied, lined the narrow road that terminated just beyond the majestic light tower. In the spring, the surrounding fields were carpeted by wildflowers in brilliant shades of purple, blue, and yellow. Lupine, Indian Paint Brush, and Baby Blue Eyes grew in abundance.

The light tower dominated the reservation. It rose 155 feet above water, its beacon visible nineteen miles out to sea; only the curvature of the earth limited its range. To ascend the cylindrical white tower, keepers climbed 145 steps to the top. From the lantern room, breathtaking views could be seen of the cliff-lined coast to the north and south. The point was the essence of rugged beauty, and in 1949, it was the domain of Bill Owens.

But days of splendor were sometimes splashed with the harsh realities of the sea. On the morning of September 9, the light station was shrouded in fog. A misty soup had mustered itself the day before, a nuance of nature that the artist or poet might have welcomed as friend but the sailor or light keeper did not. The keeper on-watch engaged the diaphone foghorn; two blasts every sixty seconds. Point Arena's fog signal characteristic—a pattern that told ships their location—was one blast three-seconds in length, silent one-second, another blast two-seconds, then silent fifty-four. A good sea captain not only knew the lay of the coastland and the literal depths of the sea, but each light station's phonetic code.

Nevertheless, both the keepers and sailors at sea knew that a foghorn's sound was conveyed in a fickle manner. At times, the blast could be heard ten miles away, and at others, only when the mariner's ship was precariously close. There were "dead zones," areas the blast of the diaphone seemed unable to penetrate.

Owens was up early that Friday, ensuring the continuous operation of the fog signal throughout the night and into the morning. The grey mist thickened and now blanketed the entire coast. Visibility had become extremely poor, less than 100 yards.

Owens was at the breakfast table sipping his morning coffee when

The Point Arena Light Station as it appeared in September 1948. The wrecked freighter Pacific Enterprise *can be seen in the distance. The Owens cottage is the closest dwelling to the tower. (Courtesy of the Michael Semas Collection)*

he first heard it: the sound of a ship's horn, bleating like a lost sheep in search of a shepherd. Between sips, he tapped his fingers on the table. Isabel knew *that* phonetic code—worry. It was just after 9 A.M.

What Owens could hear—but not see—was the British freighter *Pacific Enterprise.* The vessel was heading south from British Columbia on her return to England—a long way from home and in more ways than one. With each blast of the vessel's horn, Bill's tapping quickened.

"That ship's in too close!"

Owens raced out the front door. He flew through the gate and ran toward the light tower. The keeper was halfway there when, beyond the grey veil of fog, he heard the wrenching sound of metal grinding upon rock. Seconds of silence followed. Then he heard the sound that every keeper on the coast feared: the sustained distress-blast from the horn of a ship. The *Pacific Enterprise,* somewhere in the mist, lay as helpless as an animal caught in a trap.

PART I

Chapter One

The Early Road

As winter gave way to spring, and the calendar turned to 1900, it marked the beginning of a new century where world change would be far greater than those alive at the time could possibly imagine.

It started quickly. In 1901, an Italian electrical engineer and inventor named Guglielmo Marconi produced the initial "miracle" by sending the first radio transmission across the Atlantic Ocean using his wireless telegraph system. The message traveled 2,200 miles—from Cornwall, England to St. John's, Newfoundland.

In 1903, the Wright Brothers would achieve what had been thought to be impossible—by making man's first successful powered flight, skimming above the sand dunes at a remote spot on the Outer Banks of North Carolina called Kitty Hawk.

At the turn of the century, the birth-year of William Owens, the automobile was still considered an unreliable novelty and a passing mechanical fancy. No one had yet driven a "machine" successfully across the United States. That feat would be accomplished, also in 1903, by an adventuring thirty-one-year-old Vermont physician named Horatio Nelson Jackson.

Upon the very crest of this monumental wave of innovation, William "Bill" Owens was born December 16, 1900. Despite the stunning technological advances taking place, life in Owens' hard-scrabble state of West Virginia was tenuous. It was a harsh reality young Owens would soon find himself mired in. His father, George Owens, was a literate man who scrapped together a living as a day laborer. But at age six, young Bill would be pummeled by an unspeakable storm: his father died of tuberculosis.

The death placed George's widow, Rosa, alone in the desperate circumstance of having three children to support with no husband or income. She was forced to move the family to Louisa, Kentucky, to live with her mother, Lucy Damron. Only four years later, Rosa Owens, too, succumbed to illness. At age ten, Bill Owens was an orphan.

Now in the care of his grandmother, Bill, with his younger siblings—a sister, Minnie, and a brother, Theodore Roosevelt Owens—lacked many of life's basic necessities, food chief among them.

Seeing the strain on his grandmother to feed the three grandchildren, Bill completed the eighth grade and promptly left home. At the age of fourteen, he made his way to Huntington, West Virginia—just across the Kentucky border—and found work at a bakery. Later, the teenager worked at a lumber mill.

It's unknown whether young Owens was plagued for any length of time with despondency over his life circumstances. But he seemed to have developed a persistence during these years, a gritty nature and self-dependency that would stay with him the rest of his life. The unceasing need of finding a place to sleep—and food to eat—fostered a determined work ethic. Owens did not flinch at hard labor. Not one bit.

When, in 1917, the United States entered the World War, Bill attempted to enlist in the Army but was turned away for being under-aged. An uncle drove to a West Virginia army camp to pick him up. The following year, Bill tried enlisting again, this time in Kentucky. He gave his age as eighteen, though he was still only seventeen. His uncle let him go.

Owens enlisted on April 10, 1918. He was only five feet seven inches tall at the time and weighed all of 117 pounds. After basic training, he was assigned to the 50th Infantry; his company was shipped to France.

The war remained a brutal and bloody event until the day of Germany's surrender in 1918. The Allies and Germany fought the battles of Amines and the Marne, and the ensuing counter-offensive known as the Hundred Days Offensive.

Losses on both sides to machine gun fire and artillery were horrific. Each battlefield resembled a scene from hell, filled with dismemberment and bodies twisted in death. An estimated 9 to 15 million people died in the war.

Bill was among the lucky ones.

His only injuries came from a beating he endured at the hands of local French thugs. "One night, we were all going on liberty. And I was a little late getting dressed and shaved. I said, 'You fellows go ahead and I'll find you downtown.' When I got downtown, three or four Frenchmen jumped me, beat me up, and kicked my teeth out. I've got no use for the French."

Owens was "over there" when the peace armistice was signed in the Forest of Compiegne on November 11, 1918.

The term of Bill's service expired in September 1919. He was given an honorable discharge and he sailed home to America, arriving in Baltimore. He soon found work as an oiler on the merchant ship M.S. *Benowa*. When the *Benowa* reached San Francisco, the ship's parent company declared bankruptcy. A court order mandated the owners pay the crew members enough money to return home.

During the short time Bill was in San Francisco, the city's mild climate agreed with him. He discovered he enjoyed the West Coast's lack of humidity and temperature extremes.

To his mind, San Francisco weather was neither too cold nor hot— at least for any length of time. He hated the severe winters of the East Coast, and the humidity of the summer. By the time he had returned to Baltimore, Owens was determined to eventually find his way back to California—and this time, permanently.

———

In Easton, Maryland, near the turn of the century, Charles and Cora Leaverton would have two children. Charles farmed for a while on the Eastern Shore of Maryland near the crossroad village of Cordova. It was here that their first daughter, Blanche, was born on December 7, 1902. A second daughter, named after Cora, would follow just thirteen months later. Born January 22, 1904, the child would be called by her middle name, Isabel, the remainder of her life.

Heartbreak hounded the girls—Isabel especially. When she was nine months old her mother died of typhoid fever. Charles was overwhelmed; he was unable to both farm *and* care for the young girls. Blanche and Isabel were placed with grandparents while he continued to farm until 1911. Then, he gave it up. He moved to Baltimore and found work as a conductor for the B&O Railroad. He left Isabel and her sister with their grandparents on the farm in Cordova.

The girls rarely saw their father for the next three years. The separation from Charles Leaverton—a necessary one in his eyes but a stinging rejection in the eyes of the girls—stayed with Isabel for years.

The sense of ostracism deepened when Charles married a woman named Nola Kirby. He and his new spouse began a family, having two children of their own. Charles seemed content to live his new life in Baltimore and was apparently unbothered by the absence of his own daughters. He never asked the girls to join his second family and live with them.

At the conclusion of each school year, the sisters would visit their father at Charles and Nola's home. The girls took the train from Cordova to Claiborne on Eastern Bay, then caught a boat across the Chesapeake Bay to Baltimore. As the boat plied northward up the bay, Isabel would see the Thomas Point Shoal Lighthouse off the port side. The sisters inspected the lighthouse quizzically, Isabel thinking—she would later recall—what a lonely existence it must be for a lighthouse keeper and his family.

During their visits, their stepmother, Nola, treated the sisters as trespassers. And for reasons unknown, Nola was especially harsh with the kindly Isabel. Perhaps she was seen as a stark contrast to her own children, or maybe a threat for the affections of Charles. But Nola, it is said, rarely missed an opportunity to strike Isabel whenever they were outside the view of others. Returning to the farm at summer's end had some benefit, if only as an escape from her stepmother's abuse.

Isabel's projection of lighthouse life as "lonely" seemed reflective of a child excluded from her father and stepmother's daily lives. Such abandonment and abuse would cause others to become angry, distrustful, and bitter. Isabel, however, was none of these.

Instead, she transformed her rejection into something positive. She became an individual of notable decency—personable to others while resisting any need to criticize. And, perhaps as a means of self-confirmation, she also came to embrace hard work without complaint. Rather than allow bitterness to attach itself to her like a ball-and-chain, Isabel, the *Mendocino Beacon* would write years later, possessed "an unassuming manner and abundance of kindness."

At the age of sixteen, Isabel and Blanche decided to move to Baltimore. Isabel found work as a bookkeeper with the White Sewing Machine Company on Eutaw Street.

A year later, she met Bill Owens.

He had just returned from San Francisco and "was boarding with a family down the street from us." Bill didn't sweep her off her feet. As the Owens daughters remember Isabel saying, "He was persistent; and I admired that."

On February 4, 1922, Bill and Isabel were married. Nearly two years later, the couple had their first child, George Owens, born in December 1923. He lived only a month and died on January 5. The infant would prove to be the only son born to the couple. But he would not be the last aching loss they would experience.

———

His desire to move West never left Bill. For he and Isabel, the congestion of Baltimore had created a yearning for open space. So, in early November 1926, the couple packed their car, left their home, and headed for California. They weren't alone; in the 1920s and 1930s, the oil, agriculture, and entertainment industries attracted millions of people to California.

Bill and Isabel's collie, "Shep," rode with her head out the car window from coast to coast.

Outside of downtown San Francisco, the Bay area in 1926 was marked by rolling hills sprinkled with oak trees. There were small hamlets that dotted the train line that ran south from the city and past Leland Stanford's sprawling farm in Palo Alto that had now become Stanford University.

The Owens would settle in Visitacion Valley, a neighborhood in a southeast section of San Francisco. The town was within driving distance of the city but still retained "elbow room" and had close access to the nearby countryside. Bill soon began work as a plumber and pipefitter at the Bethlehem Shipyard in San Francisco.

Over the next four years, three daughters were born to the couple. Shirley, the oldest, arrived in 1927. Then came Sarah a year later. And in 1930, Dixie was born.

Isabel and Bill Owens outside their home in Visitacion Valley, California in 1929. Isabel holds daughter Sarah while Bill holds Shirley. (Courtesy of Owens Family)

On Sundays, Bill often went to Angel Island across the bay toward Tiberon. There, the fishing was good. And when he heard Carl Reit's description of the lighthouse keeper's duties, he could think of little else. Soon, the chain of events began that would bring Owens to the Custom House offices—and to a face-to-face encounter with Lighthouse Superintendent Harry W. Rhodes.

The now "former-pipefitter" resigned from Bethlehem Shipyard with the best wishes and congratulations of his supervisor. By the evening of August 5, 1931, Bill and Isabel were packed and ready.

Chapter Two

The Engineer and the Captain

Couples picnicking along the shores of America in the 1900s rarely gave a second thought to the sight of a ship's bleached bones from a long-ago wreck, now half-buried by wind-driven sand. The relic was considered a charming enhancement to the surroundings—with little reflection given to the tragic events that hurled the schooner on the rocks and reefs. Folks found the sun too pleasant. The sand too warm. And the conversation too comfortable.

But the hours and minutes that led those ships to sink or shatter against the coastline were ones of trauma, struggle, and death.

A need to provide some measure of safeguard for the sailors at sea had existed almost as long as civilized man had been around. Ancient efforts to protect vessels began as bonfires on coastal hilltops. Later, in the time of the destruction of Babylon in 650 B.C., the first light source to be regularly maintained for sailors was established.

In the third century, B.C., the Lighthouse of Alexandria was built in Egypt. It is considered one of the "Seven Wonders of the Ancient World." The tower rose at least 330 feet in height and was lit at the apex by a reflecting mirror during the day and a fire by night. The spectacular structure, ninety-eight feet square at its base, stood above the harbor for more than a thousand years before a series of earthquakes caused the mighty tower to gradually collapse beginning in 956 A.D.

The modern lighthouse era began in the 1700s when commerce exploded on the open seas. It occurred along the coasts of Europe and across the Atlantic to the shores of North America. Eddystone Lighthouse, ten miles off the Cornwall coast of England, was a major advancement in the design of the modern lighthouse. It was built upon a reef and the engineer, Britain's John Smeaton, implemented revolutionary new concepts during construction. He used granite blocks with dovetailed joints and hydraulic lime, a form of cement capable of setting well—even under water. The tower tapered toward the top and, over time, demonstrated excellent structural stability.

The effectiveness of the actual light lagged. First, wood was burned, then coal. Oil lamps and candles followed. Eddystone Light used an arrangement of twenty-four candles until 1810.

All light sources faced severe limits in the distance from which the light could be seen. And, of course, the shorter the distance between light and ship, the less effective a lighthouse would be. A ship needed as much warning as possible to avoid the often-rocky dangers lurking near the lighthouse. And that meant seeing it from the greatest distance possible.

Discovering how to magnify the light source became the new technological focus. A Swiss scientist, Aime Argand, invented a device in 1781 that, for a time, became the standard for lighthouse lumination. The lamp held a candle within a cylindrical sleeve and was cupped by a parabolic reflector. This combination of the curved reflecting disk and light produced the Argand Lamp and marked a significant step forward.

But within forty years, a young Frenchman would create a lens so technologically advanced that the physics of the lens design remain in use today. His name was Augustin Fresnel. He was a trained engineer, but also a physicist and mathematician.

Despite the resentment Bill Owens maintained of the French, the light keeper allowed for one significant exception. He admired Fresnel and his invention of the compound lens design that eventually bore his name.

Although the physics behind the lens would have been unfamiliar to Owens, the light keeper knew full-well the excellence of the optics in collecting and magnifying light. To Owens, the lens was a masterpiece.

Often described as a "giant beehive" that surrounded a single lamp, the Fresnel lens (pronounced Fruh-NELL), was the product of years of scientific study by the French engineer. Prior to his work, most scientists agreed with Isaac Newton's theory that light was a collection of particles. But Fresnel determined that light behaved as a wave.

Considered controversial at first, Fresnel's research in optics led to the acceptance of the wave theory of light. He composed mathematical formulas to explain optical phenomena and discovered nuances of light polarization, diffraction, and refraction.

Fresnel was born in Normandy, France, in 1788, one of four children to Jacques and Augustine Fresnel. Health problems plagued him throughout his life; he was thin, frail, and had a long, gaunt face that descended into a narrow, pointed chin. His hair was a jumbled collection of dark waves that strayed in every direction.

Fresnel was home-schooled until the age of twelve, and during that time, demonstrated no penchant for science. Then, he began his formal studies and proceeded to excel in science and mathematics. In 1804, Augustin was accepted into Ecole Polytechnique. He graduated two years later and enrolled at Ecole Nationale des Ponts et Chaussees (National School of Bridges and Roads). By 1809, he had graduated in engineering and began a career constructing roads.

But the making of roadways proved to be of little interest to him. What fascinated Fresnel was the subject of light and optics. Every free moment, it seemed, he devoted to the study of how beams of light behaved.

In 1819, he received the "Grand Prix" of the Academy of Sciences for his dissertation on diffraction and the wave theory of light. Soon, he began investigations on the effect of glass prisms for use in lenses as an amplifier of light.

His work led to the invention of the
Fresnel lens. Introduced in 1822, the spectacular lens—both in appearance and func-
tion—would become the gold standard of
light projection in lighthouses around the
world. By the 1830s, scientists and engineers agreed, "the brilliancy of the beam of
light formed by these lenses has never been
surpassed in lighthouses."

Fresnel wasn't the first to use lenses in

Augustin Fresnel

lighthouses. Thomas Rogers, a glass cutter,
is considered to have suggested this in 1788 to Trinity House—England's authority of lighthouses. And in the United States, the use of lenses
began in 1810. But these efforts had proved less than satisfactory due to
the diffusion—or spreading—of light beams.

Fresnel noted that light rays aren't parallel to one another. The further away from the light source the rays get, the further apart they get
from one another. That's why light appears fainter the further one gets
from the light source. This was the problem Fresnel was trying to solve.

The engineer realized there were two ways to alter light direction. The
first was called "reflection," when light *bounces off* an object such as a mirror. The second was "refraction," when the light *passes through* an object,
such as water or glass, and changes direction.

Fresnel knew that light is refracted at the point at which it passes
from one medium to another—in the case of his lens, from air to glass
and back to air again. He found the curved surface of the glass prisms
could focus the light in any desired direction. Extra prisms were added
to the top and bottom of the lens so it could "catch" and redirect more
light. High-quality glass was used in both prisms and bullseyes.

The Fresnel lens took the light, and, as never before, collected it in
one unified direction. The concentric rings were actually "steps" (thick
ridges) in the lens surface. Each step would bend the light slightly more
than the one beneath it, resulting in the light rays all emerging in a perfect, parallel beam. A single, small light source—even a candle—became
a spotlight. The bullseye panels in the middle of the lens focused it into

a highly magnified and concentrated beam.

Fresnel had solved the problem of diffusion. His design was recognized as a quantum leap forward in technology and effectiveness, collecting over 90 percent of the light and directing it seaward in a focused beam. His lens would later be called "the invention that saved a million ships."

The scientist then designed a series of lenses built in all shapes and sizes. Originally, they were divided into four "orders" based on size, refracting power, and focal length. Later, more sizes were added, from the largest "first-order" all the way to the smallest "sixth-order" lens.

Some were gigantic. The first-order lens stood about eight and one-half feet in height—or taller. Lighthouses located on major seacoast promontories were fitted with first-order lenses to warn ships far out to sea. For use on inter-harbor waterways or small bays, the sixth-order lenses— eighteen inches in height—were utilized.

Fresnel then created a rotating apparatus, an advancement that allowed a lighthouse to not only illuminate, but to signal, as well. While a "fixed" lens showed a steady light across the horizon, a rotating lens could produce a flash.

Lighthouses came to use a series of flashes—and sometimes different-colored glass panels—to identify themselves so sea captains could confirm their locations. Like a fingerprint, the time-span of the flashes and darkness gave each light a unique means of identification—called a "light characteristic." As the beam rotated across the ocean it looked to a ship like it was flashing. The light, of course, was always on. It was merely the rotation of the lens that gave the mariner the brilliant flashing effect. A captain at sea could time the light flash and the span of darkness, called the "eclipse." That allowed him to identify which lighthouse he was seeing—like a phone number, each had its identity—and where his ship was located in relation to the light.

Prior to electricity, the rotating lens was powered by a clockwork mechanism. This involved a mechanical system—similar to a grandfather clock—where a cylindrical lead weight was attached to thick wire cable wrapped around a drum. The drum and clockwork contained a series of gears. Their "ratio" determined the speed at which the lens would rotate. Once wound, the weight would slowly lower through an opening in the tower's floor to the watch room below.

The light source and lens were the very heartbeat of each light station and were to be carefully protected. The lens' fragile glass prisms could break easily. Keepers took great care every time they were near the lens to avoid scratching a prism—or worse. Prisms were so expensive one was rarely replaced if broken.

The lens Fresnel devised has not been surpassed. Cheaper and easier-to-operate optics were eventually developed, but none exceeded Fresnel's effective projection of light upon the waterways.

———

The name of Fresnel was familiar to every California light keeper from the time lights were first installed here in 1854. To keepers from 1912 to 1939, another name was every bit as familiar—Captain Harry W. Rhodes. He was Superintendent of the Lighthouse Service's 18th District and the state's nearly fifty light stations and lightships. Each keeper's life, including that of Bill Owens, was indelibly impacted by Rhodes.

He was the undisputed sovereign of the 18th District. The hiring and promotion of personnel, beyond Bill's "congressional assist," was determined by Harry Rhodes. A light keeper's work efficiency was evaluated by Rhodes. His light station was inspected by Rhodes. If he applied for leave, it needed to be approved by Rhodes. And should the keeper wish to have family or friends visit the station, that request, too, would be granted or denied by Rhodes.

Rhodes was described as frugal and strict. Light keepers loved to tell the story when a dozen pencils were requisitioned by a light station—and thirteen were accidentally sent. Harry Rhodes requested the extra pencil be returned. True or not, old-timers swore by it.

Rhodes was a man of high standards who demanded excellence from those who worked in his district. It was these very standards Superintendent Rhodes expected of others, as well as of himself, that contributed significantly to the outstanding reputation held by the department—even if it came imbued with his sense of fastidiousness.

One keeper's wife remembered Rhodes as "a distinguished looking man." He always seemed to be in a suit, tie, and vest—often topped by a hat. He had white hair and wore starched collared shirts. With his neatly trimmed goatee, he was sometimes referred to as "Billy Goat Rhodes," though never to his face.

Upon joining the United States Lighthouse Service in 1912, the captain proved to be an able administrator from the start. Rhodes was brilliant—and accomplished in his own right. He had graduated in civil engineering from the University of California, Berkeley in 1894. After four years conducting a general practice in hydraulic engineering, he became a field officer for the United States Geodetic Survey.

During his fourteen years with the USGS, Rhodes conducted hydrographic, topographic, magnetic, and geodetic surveys on the Pacific, Atlantic, and Gulf coasts, the Panama Canal Zone, and the Hawaiian and Philippine islands.

He was also a master mariner, which is why he was known as "Captain Rhodes," though not everyone understood that seafaring connection. Between 1898 and 1912, he had spent ten seasons in Alaska commanding U.S. ships in survey work. In 1908, he made the first

Harry W. Rhodes, Superintendent of the 18th Lighthouse District, at his Custom House office in San Francisco. (Courtesy of Point Arena Light Keepers)

accurate determination of the position and elevation of Mt. McKinley.

But he and his wife, Harriet, now had a young family and Rhodes wanted work that would keep him in one place and closer to home. With that request, he was transferred to the U.S. Lighthouse Service in 1912 as an inspector for the 18th Lighthouse District.

From his home in Berkeley, Harry would drive each morning to the Oakland Pier and take the ferry *Berkeley* across the bay. It was a short walk after disembarking at the Ferry Building to reach his office at Custom House.

Each day, the *Berkeley* passed by Yerba Buena Island where the 18th District had its main supply depot for the lighthouses and lightships of California. The YBI depot stored everything necessary for their operation and maintenance: buoys, lenses, lamps, wicks, glass chimneys, oil, coal, fog-signal mechanisms, boilers, fire hoses, and every kind of building and cleaning supply required for repairs.

The Lighthouse Service needed skilled workers beyond the light keepers. YBI was home to such other employees—mechanics, carpenters, electricians, boat builders, boat captains, machinists, and blacksmiths.

One of the requirements for a light keeper was a trade skill. Electricians, carpenters, plumbers, machinists, or, ostensibly as with Bill Owens, pipefitters had an advantage in the hiring process. They could be expected to perform basic repairs around the light station. If fixes of a more complicated nature arose, a work crew would be sent out from YBI.

Each of these employees worked for Harry Rhodes once he became the chief in 1920. That year, he had 300 men under him, including keepers of major lights, YBI workers and specialists, and the crews of three light ships to help keep vessels from running aground on California's 1,264-mile coastline.

The captain never fully relinquished the role of inspector. He made it a point to visit the District's lighthouses and "see for himself" the state and running condition of the stations. At remote lighthouse reservations that could only be reached and resupplied by ships called lighthouse tenders, Harry accompanied the crew at various times and conducted inspections.

Seeing how deep and wide the Captain's influence reached makes it more understandable why he initially bristled at Congressman Welch's suggestion—or insistence—that Owens be hired. The 18th District was his kingdom—and he was king. To have an outlier such as Welch petitioning Rhodes, even as a Congressman, naturally piqued his stubbornness. And yet if Rhodes was a complicated blend of "pride" and "control," few argued that he ran a tight ship and made those around him better.

The operating base for the tenders was Yerba Buena Island. When isolated stations like Point Conception and Point Sur—or offshore stations like Anacapa or Farallon Island—required resupply, the lighthouse tenders loaded needed goods and equipment at YBI's depot. They were the workhorses of the 18th District.

Whenever Rhodes was aboard a Lighthouse Service ship, the vessel flew the superintendent of lighthouses pennant—a rectangular flag with a blue border and blue lighthouse on a white background. If a station was scheduled for an inspection, the presence of the superintendent's flag flying from a staff announced Rhodes was aboard. And lighthouse personnel had better be prepared.

The head keeper was supposed to inspect all the quarters once a week, but few did. Major inspections of the light station, where Captain Rhodes might be expected to participate, occurred once a year. These visits were dreaded by lighthouse staff and their families—and with good reason.

The Captain's inspections included everything. In addition to the light tower, lens, fog signal, lamps, coal sheds, and all machinery on the lighthouse reservation, Rhodes examined the keeper's dwellings—the cleanliness of living rooms, kitchens, bathrooms, and bedrooms. Storage sheds, garages, grounds, cisterns, and the windmills that pumped water to the homes were all, Rhodes believed, essential to the functioning of the station—and worthy of his scrutiny.

Word had long spread throughout the District about Rhodes' visits and inspections. "He would wear white gloves and run his hand over countertops," Isabel said. "We had heard he had been known to look in closets and inside chest drawers. Or even rub his gloved-hand over the walls—but he never did that with us."

The head keeper would be informed a short time before inspection, usually three to four days prior. The women on the station would clean the kitchen stove with stove polish. "And if the inspectors didn't get there before lunch to check it, then we didn't eat." Then she added with a laugh: "We didn't want to mess up that stove."

Later, when lighthouses came under the control of the United States Coast Guard, inspectors often gave only a one-day notice, a brief time of warning that would stress every former Lighthouse Service family across the country, including the Owens family.

Part II

Chapter Three

California's Elbow

On the morning of Thursday, August 6, 1931, the Owens family left San Francisco for Point Conception. The couple's three children, along with Shep, bounced excitedly up and down in the back seat of the Hudson Motor Car as they left Visitacion Valley.

Shirley, Sarah, and Dixie—ages four, three, and one—were too young to realize how their lives would be forever changed on this day. But for Bill and Isabel, the excitement of his new career with the United States Lighthouse Service was hardly containable. The future was full of promise.

The long drive to Lompoc, nestled in the hills fifty-four miles north of Santa Barbara, was brimming with conversations of optimism and uncertainty. What awaited them, they could not know, including how profoundly isolated Point Conception was in 1931—and remains today. Lompoc, the nearest town, was twenty-eight miles away.

It was late afternoon when the family reached the small Southern

Point Conception Lighthouse. Note the closed linen drapes to protect the lens during daylight hours. (Courtesy of the U.S. Coast Guard)

Pacific Depot of *Concepcion*, which used the Spanish spelling of the word. Bill spoke with the station master—the only attendant on site.

The station master, his face weathered like driftwood, told Bill to "cross the tracks and follow the trail. It will take you to the lighthouse reservation one mile that way," as he pointed westward.

Soon, they entered the lighthouse reservation's gate and made the gentle climb to the top of the hill. A man walked out of a large white duplex to greet them.

Richard George, the Head Keeper, shook Bill's hand and accepted his papers to report for duty. Mr. George, as he was referred to, had been at Point Conception since 1916 and knew every nuance of the lighthouse and property.

Point Conception was a four-man station. There was a head keeper, and three assistants--ranking in seniority from first to third. Owens was the new man, and third assistant.

Since it was late, Mr. and Mrs. George had the Owens family spend the night with them. They could set up their house in the morning.

From the duplex, Bill and Isabel could see the light and lens he would be trained to operate and maintain. Down the hill on the ocean side was a small mesa. The light tower, with its thick walls and first-order lens, stood prominently to the left.

A wooden stairway led straight down the hill. Near the lower landing was a cottage, the third assistant keeper's quarters—only twenty yards northward of the light tower. The stairway, like a long-descending line of dominoes, made for a challenging trek of 185 steps. For that reason, trips up and down were economized as much as possible.

Further down from the light was the fog-signal building, a coal house, and a carpenter shop. Right of the stairs, a chute ran from the top of the hill to the bottom, ending at the supply shed. Stores and provisions of

The 1881 lighthouse was built on a mesa below the hilltop. The fog-signal building is closest to the point. The Owens home can be seen bottom right. (Courtesy of U.S. Coast Guard)

lighter weight could be slid down. Heavy items, including the Owens' furniture, would be lowered slowly utilizing a rope, block, and tackle attached to a horse.

Like all other buildings on the lighthouse reservation, the Owens' home was painted white with a light brown trim, or, as the Lighthouse Service called it, "lead trim." Each structure was topped with a red roof.

The family was anxious to see their new home the next morning. It had a large kitchen, a large living room, two bedrooms, a bathroom, and a screened-in porch. There was also a large, coal-fueled cooking stove. On the farm in Maryland, Isabel had learned to cook with wood. In Baltimore, they used gas. This would be more challenging. "The coal," she said, "made so much ash the stove had to be cleaned every morning before I started a new fire."

The stove was not only where meals were prepared, it was also where hot water was generated for the family. A hot-water tank had been installed beside the stove with pipes running through the fire box. There was plenty of hot water to meet family needs—so long as the fire was burning.

There were few neighbors at Point Conception. The Cojo Ranch hands and the Southern Pacific section crew that maintained the tracks were about it. There were no electric lights or telephones either. The station wouldn't go electric for another seventeen years, 1948.

While the Owens family lived at Conception, clothes were cleaned, at least early on, using a glass washboard instead of a washing machine. Ironing was done with Sad Irons, a flat-bottomed triangular "smoother" that Isabel heated on the stove. The family used kerosene lamps for light.

As the weeks passed, the family settled in. Isabel learned how to order groceries from Lompoc. Each family on the station traded with the same store. When the dirt road through the Cojo Ranch was muddied by rain, the lighthouse personnel had to depend on the train, sending in a written order for supplies. The grocer would box them up and ship them out by rail the next day. The boxed groceries would be lowered down the chute. "We couldn't send heavy items down that way," Isabel said. "They'd gather too much speed and crash into the storage shed at the bottom."

The girls had a fenced-in back yard in which to play. Before long, Bill had constructed a swing set and teeter-totter for his daughters. The children also had the family dog, Shep, who followed the girls about the station as if she were leashed to them.

———

To the Chumash Indians, Point Conception is the most sacred site in California. For many centuries, they knew the point as the "Western Gate" where all new life entered the world and from where all souls departed for the west after death. They still believe it to be a "power place." It is here that the Chumash believe they hear the voices of their ancestors who long inhabited the land. Today, among archeologists, there is agreement that at least five villages have existed on this site over the last 7,000 years.

In more recent centuries, explorers in sailing ships, and later, sailors in steamers, also knew Point Conception to have a connection with "the departed." The place had acquired a reputation for shipwrecks and loss of life. Here, there is the confluence of two strong offshore currents, the California Current, which flows south, and the deeper Davidson Current, which flows north. The Davidson produces a counter-current— generating rough seas and an enormous, turbulent eddy off the point. Combined with the wildly escalating winds through Gaviota Pass, the seas off Conception had earned its well-deserved nickname, "The Graveyard of the Pacific."

The *Pacific Coast Pilot*—the mariner's handbook of depths, currents, and anchorages— contained a warning to ship captains: "A marked change of climatic and meteorological conditions is experienced off the point, the transition often being remarkably sudden and well defined."

It is here California's coastline makes a sharp southeastward turn, forming the Santa Barbara Channel. From Conception, the shoreline travels east to Ventura, then descends toward San Diego at a forty-five-degree angle. In thick weather or heavy seas, the port-turn to enter the channel can be easily miscalculated—with tragic consequences.

One such error occurred on the evening of September 8, 1923, eight years before Bill arrived at Conception. It happened fifteen miles north

of the point at a place known as "The Honda" and resulted in the greatest peacetime loss of U.S. Navy ships in the nation's history.

Destroyer Squadron Eleven had been steaming south from San Francisco to San Diego under the command of Capt. Edward Watson. The
ships encountered heavy fog. But due to the nature of the exercise—
simulating wartime conditions—the squadron did not slow. Thinking
they had reached the Santa Barbara Channel, Watson and the navigator
turned east to course 095.

The destroyers used a method of navigation common at the time
called "dead reckoning." The navigator depended on three points of
information, the ship's compass heading, the ship's speed, and the time
spent on each heading and at each speed. Given this information, the
navigator could calculate the route and distance his ship had traveled.

The flagship USS *Delphy* was equipped with a radio navigation
receiver, but it was new technology and not yet trusted. Her captain,
Lieutenant Commander Hunter, believed the bearings to be in error.
Despite the heavy fog, Watson ordered the destroyers to follow in close
formation. Believing themselves to be eight miles offshore, the ships
steered by the lights of the vessel ahead.

Minutes after 9 P.M. the first ship, the *Delphy*, rammed into rocks
at twenty knots. She immediately sounded her siren to alert ships in the
column. But six others followed and were wrecked on the jagged rocks.
The destroyers *S.P. Lee, Young, Woodbury, Nicholas, Fuller, Delphy,* and
Chauncy were all lost that night; twenty-three men died.

Rescue efforts began quickly. Light keepers from nearby Point
Arguello rigged up breeches buoys from atop the bluff to haul men to
safety. Nearby fishermen plucked sailors from the wrecked ships. The
five destroyers that avoided wrecking lowered lifeboats to rescue crew
members from the doomed destroyers.

The *Young* suffered the worst of it. Her hull was torn open. Water
gushed through her punctured sides. Twenty men drowned while
trapped below her decks.

The following day, the outlines of the seven destroyers, twisted and
half-submerged, could be seen through the fog, impaled upon the rocks
called the Devil's Jaw.

The Honda Point Disaster. The **Young** *lay capsized in the center while the* **Delphy,** *broken in two, is seen at the bottom. A life raft and observers are visible at lower right.*

The Board of Inquiry determined the Honda Point disaster was the fault of squadron commander Watson and two others in his command. "In the opinion of the court," the report said, "the disaster is directly attributable to bad errors and faulty navigation on the part of three officers attached to and serving on the *Delphy*, viz: the squadron commander, the commanding officer, and the navigating officer ... Their responsibility is complete, and the court sees no extenuating circumstances."

Eleven officers were court-martialed. All were acquitted except for Capt. Edward Watson and Lt. Comdr. Donald Hunter, commander of the *Delphy*. Of the three "responsible officers," the *Delphy's* navigator was cleared on charges of negligence. Watson and Hunter were convicted and stripped of their seniority.

Amid the crisis, inspirational conduct had been exhibited by Navy and lighthouse personnel. The few local residents also responded admirably. One notable example was Mrs. James Thompson, a farmer's wife on a lonely wind-swept ranch eight miles from the scene. Her name, wrote the *Los Angeles Evening Post*, "was the toast of the fleet. For it was she who was the first to 'mother' the half-drowned sailors."

Continued the *Evening Post*:

> Hearing the shrieking of the sirens from the disabled vessels, she hastily dressed and, going out, rang the old ranch bell to summon all the ranch hands. "Something has happened at Honda," she said.
>
> Quickly, all the bedding and clothing on the ranch was piled into an ancient automobile. Coffee and provisions—everything the ranch had—was put in and with the ranch hands as company, she set out for the treacherous shore.
>
> Reaching the site, in the car lights began to appear, dimly through the fog, hundreds of "gobs," cold, shivering, many without clothing and suffering from exposure. She set up camp by the water's edge. Half-frozen sailors, exhausted from their battle with the sea, were given blankets, as long as there were any, and steaming coffee soon arrived.

Thompson then sent a ranch hand back with the automobile to rouse the settlement of Honda—a handful of houses and a few stores. "Every blanket in the place was brought to the shore along with ample provisions," the *Long Beach Press Telegram* reported.

"She's the mother of the fleet," was the word the sailors passed down the line as they left. "The simple little farm woman," wrote the newspaper, "received more kisses than she could count from 'the boys' before they entrained [for San Diego]."

———

Back at the light station, Bill Owens had heard plenty of stories from his co-workers of the shipwrecks that had plagued Point Conception. His job now was to learn to operate the aids to navigation that could protect ships passing through the region. It was purely on-the-job training. And there was much to learn.

There also existed a protocol to adapt to, one that was quasi-military in nature. All communication passed through the head keeper. Letters to and from the District Office were addressed "through the Head Keeper." Requests of all kinds—sick leave, vacation, or permission for visitors to stay at the station—passed through him.

Present, too, was a culture of formality. The head keeper and his wife were addressed as "Mr. and Mrs. George." This was so with all the keepers and wives. Only between the men themselves were first names used.

Bill's first lesson was that a keeper is "on-watch" twenty-four hours a day at the station. Watch-shifts rotated between men every four hours (evening) to six hours (daytime).

The operation of the light was only a portion of the watch duties; the light normally operated only from sunset to sunrise. But fog offered the abnormal. It was among a ship captain's greatest hazards and could appear at any time. When the man on-watch observed weather conditions that could limit visibility, especially rolling fog, the foghorn was quickly engaged. There was no time—day or night—when these two essential aids to navigation could be left unattended.

Beyond those primary tasks, Bill learned the other jobs that needed minding. And there were many.

Repairs of all kinds had to be performed; if anything broke, the keepers fixed it. They maintained the mechanical equipment. Buildings were constantly cleaned and swept. Care and maintenance of cisterns and windmills for their water needs could not be neglected. The eight-foot Fresnel lens needed to be cleaned and

Bill and Isabel Owens behind the head keeper's duplex at Point Conception, circa 1932. (Courtesy of the Owens Family)

polished, mantles trimmed and replaced, and coal oil levels monitored and refilled.

There were thick windows around the "gallery" to be washed and dried each day and protective curtains to draw around the lens when the light was extinguished in the morning. There was station property to be picked up and tours to be given during visiting hours (though this was seldom required here, given Conception's isolation). There was plenty of painting to be done—sheds, fences, outer buildings, and barns. And if the light tower itself needed painting, the keepers did the whitewashing.

Bill knew this was to be accomplished in all weather—rain, gales, storms, and more—the very conditions that were most hazardous to ships at sea. The hours were both long and grueling.

But Owens had found his "place" in the Lighthouse Service. He liked the work. He liked the setting. And he liked the significance of the job. Coastal commerce relied on the safe transportation of goods upon the sea. Every ship and mariner depended on the life-saving aids-to-navigation the light stations provided.

In short, his new profession mattered.

Point Conception Light Station was situated on about thirty acres of land in Santa Barbara County. Even as early as 1850, the federal government had been convinced of the need to build West Coast lighthouses. And Conception already possessed a deadly reputation among mariners. On September 28 of that year, Congress passed a bill to construct eight lighthouses on the Pacific Coast. Seven of the lights were to be built in California, the other at Cape Disappointment in Washington. Point Conception was among those authorized.

At that time, the agency responsible for the nation's lighthouses was the United States Lighthouse Establishment. The director, or "Fifth Auditor," was Stephen Pleasanton. He had gained some acclaim by saving important government documents when the British attacked and burned Washington, D.C., during the War of 1812.

President James Monroe, worried at the prospect of a British attack on the capital, assigned Pleasanton to preserve state papers, including the Articles of Confederation, the United States Constitution, and the Declaration of Independence. Pleasanton did this by whisking the documents to Leesburg, Virginia, thirty-five miles away, where he hid them in an abandoned stone house.

Now, in 1850, Pleasanton was being heavily criticized for his handling of the lighthouses and their equipment. Mariners and merchants across the West were desperate for the construction of lighthouses. The Transcontinental Railroad was still decades from completion; virtually all commerce relied on ocean vessels.

The eight lighthouses Pleasanton authorized would be built with the same blueprint, a Cape-Cod-style tower rising from its center. The building plans, however, were inadequate for several of the locations selected, including Point Conception. Worse, the buildings were designed to display the Argand lamps and parabolic reflectors—favored by Pleasanton because of their low cost. But the Fresnel lens, by now accepted as the world's finest optic engineering, had been available for over ten years and far exceeded the Argand system in effectiveness.

Construction at Conception was completed by the summer of 1854, but it proved useless. A major in the Army Corp of Engineers, Hartman Bache, inspected the new light and found the brick mortar already crumbling and several gutter troughs missing—blown away from the roof. Adding to his consternation, Bache also discovered the lantern room was too small in diameter to accommodate the first-order Fresnel lens that was now on its way from Paris to replace the system Pleasanton had chosen.

Bache ordered the lighthouse rebuilt from the ground up.

The new building, completed the next year, stood 220 feet above sea level. In October 1855, the Fresnel lens arrived by ship and was offloaded at the Cojo Anchorage. On the night of February 1, 1856, the tower at Point Conception first beamed a flash of light across the Pacific.

Over the next two decades, the lighthouse sustained mild damage during major earthquakes that struck at Fort Tejon and Hayward. The settling foundation and water damage to the tower added further to its deterioration. A Lighthouse Board inspection determined the tower and dwelling to be in poor condition and proposed a third light tower be constructed at Conception. Since the light had often been obscured by the high coastal fog, plans were made for the new tower to be built at a lower level.

This one would be built halfway down the hill on the mesa. The improved plans and drawings for the new light tower were prepared under the direction of Lt. Col. R.S. Williamson, an officer with the U.S. Army Corp of Engineers.

In 1882, the new tower was completed, and the first-order lens was remounted. A cottage for the third assistant keeper and additional out-buildings were also finished. A wooden shed and store house were placed near the keeper's cottage and a flight of stairs was built from the top of the hill to the new tower.

On June 20, 1882, the new light first shone.

The revolving first-order Fresnel lens itself stood seven-and-one-half feet tall. The spectacular glass-prismed lens magnified the lamp's light to 340,000 candlepower. It had sixteen panels, flashed a beam of light every thirty seconds, and could be seen twenty miles to sea.

Half a century later, the Owens family settled into their surroundings. Just down the hill from the tower at Point Conception, the property had a low wood-railed fence lining the bluffs. The cliffs themselves were fifty feet in height—higher still as the hill rose eastward—with a steep drop-off in every direction. The face of the bluffs had the appearance of a hundred pancakes stacked upon each other—layered marine strata that testified of California's underwater past. Caves pocketed the waterline and when large swells charged in, they struck with such force a thunderous "whump" boomed across the station. "Even the ground would shake," said Owens.

Planked walkways with handrails linked each building. The men found the railings useful in the darkness to safely reach the fog signal—especially so when the wind was howling. During late night watches, a keeper entering the fog-signal building alone sometimes had the uneasy

Though mostly unseen by the family, the layered strata of the bluffs below the light tower were magnificent. Note the protective fences. (Courtesy of the Owens Family)

sense that someone else was there. It was an eerie feeling that was hard to shake.

Whenever the Owens girls ventured beyond the gates of the house, Shep would follow. If they wandered too close to the cliffs for the dog's comfort, she'd back them up.

The front door to the house was on the ocean side. Isabel had been told not to use it. During rough weather, waves crashed into the cliffs below with tremendous force. It sounded like "explosions" to Isabel, and towering walls of sea spray were blown over the bluff and onto the buildings. If the front door wasn't tightly sealed, salt water seeped in.

The back door, at the rear of the screened porch, was the entry everyone commonly used. There was a small yard on that side of the house, as well, with a white picket fence and gate surrounding the quarters.

The setting was beautiful, isolated, and with young children, precarious. A degree of "protective alert" was always necessary for the Owens family. Isabel learned that lesson one sunny afternoon while sitting in the living room reading the *Saturday Evening Post*. The two older girls,

The Owens family with Shep in 1934. The girls from left to right are Shirley, Dixie, Jean, Joan, and Sarah. (Courtesy of Owens family)

Shirley and Sarah, were playing in the fenced yard toward the ocean. The youngest, Dixie, was outside the back porch by the picket fence.

Soon, their mother heard a strange sound, a rattling sound like paper being wadded up. The sound would start and stop every few seconds. Isabel walked outside to investigate. She saw Dixie standing in the gateway, her face flush with fear. She was staring at an enormous rattlesnake, coiled and shaking its tail. Like a flash of lightning, it lunged at the little girl. As the snake struck forward, its head stopped abruptly, blocked by the palings of the gate. The serpent's head was so large it couldn't fit through the gap. It recoiled to strike again. Isabel quickly swooped Dixie up and whisked her away.

Bill was working atop the hill when Isabel called on the intercom.

"Bill, Bill, we've got a rattler at our gate!"

"Get my gun ready and hand it to me over the fence!"

He raced down the 185 steps. As he reached the house, Isabel was waiting with the shotgun, loaded and ready. Bill spotted the coiled snake, emptied both barrels, and the threat to his family was dead.

But that evening—after Dixie's narrow escape from the poisonous fangs of the rattler—the Owens' remoteness from town seemed even further, and more dangerous, than ever.

And that danger, time would prove, wasn't going away.

Chapter Four

Ships in the Fog

The head keeper, Mr. George, owned the horse and buggy at the station. For the Georges to make a trip to town was a two-day journey. After reaching Lompoc, getting a bite to eat and shopping, the Georges would need a hotel for the evening. Consequently, journeys to town were rare.

But with the Owens family having a car, the only one on-station, that would change. The families began to make the journey once a month. Even with the many ranch gates to open and close, the round trip could now be easily made in a day. "The Lighthouse Service gave us six-hours one-day-a-week to go to town and do your shopping," Bill said. "And if you used seven, one hour come off your annual leave. The head keeper kept track of your hours when you logged in and out."

Mrs. George was delighted by the convenience of the Owens car and often traveled to town with Bill and Isabel. Isabel had not yet learned to drive, despite their family owning what Bill believed to be the first car at the station.

In 1932, Bill had bought lottery tickets during a visit to San Francisco. To the amazement of everyone at the light station, he won a thousand dollars. And he knew just how he wanted to spend it.

"He got in the old Hudson and headed for Lompoc to buy a new car," said Isabel. "And it caught fire before he got it to Lompoc. We always kidded him about it; he rode it so hard he burned it up before he got it to town."

Decades later, in an interview, Bill waited for Isabel's laughter to subside.

"No. Tell you what happened. Had a big Hudson—about the size of a box car. It caught on *far*," he said with his Kentucky accent. "Tell you the reason it caught on *far*. There'd been a wreck a little bit before I reached Lompoc. There was a sump in the road and it was full of gasoline. Well, I come in there and I slammed the brakes on. The car skid and threw sparks in that sump and set the gasoline off. So, I just let it burn.

While on vacation, Bill poses at an auto court in front of his Hudson Motor Car. (Courtesy of Owens Family)

Didn't even try to put it out."

Some debate exists over Bill's "first car" claim. In the early 1900s, a man named Harley Weeks was a keeper at Point Conception. His son, Harry, recalled an assistant who came briefly to the light station, a man who had purchased an automobile from the REO Motor Car Company. It had been delivered by train to the Southern Pacific Depot at nearby Concepcion.

Weeks said the new car "could not make it up the hill" and had to be pulled by mules to the station. The only place he could drive it was on the hard-packed sand of a beach near the station. The lighthouse mules had to haul it down and back on each occasion.

Bill's car may, therefore, have been the first car *driven* on and off the station, a distinction that may well have satisfied him.

Owens and his car made another "first" at Conception.

Captain Rhodes had notified the station he would be arriving by tender on a certain date and wanted someone to meet him with a car. At the appointed time and date, Bill drove to Cojo Cove to meet Rhodes. Bill could see the tender sitting offshore. But the ocean was choppy, rough enough that Rhodes had second thoughts about attempting to land at the cove in a launch boat. He never made it in; the tender lifted anchor and continued down the coast.

"I got back to the station," said Bill, savoring a favorite recollection, "and decided to put in a bill to him for mileage. It was only one mile." Bill smiled. "I got a personal check from him."

It was likely the first—and shortest—mileage claim ever submitted to Captain Rhodes from a keeper at Conception.

By the end of 1932, Bill and Isabel decided the girls were getting too big for their beds. The two youngest, Sarah and Dixie, were now four and two years of age and had been sleeping in cribs. On a trip to San Francisco, Bill ordered three single beds to be sent to Conception. They gave one crib away, keeping the other "just in case."

It was a wise move. Several months later, Isabel found she was pregnant.

When Isabel was five months pregnant, the family decided to take a week-long vacation to Los Angeles and visit friends Mary and Lloyd

Nunn. It was March 1933, and their timing of the visit could hardly have been worse. In the early evening of March 10, a major earthquake ripped across the Newport-Inglewood fault.

Isabel first heard a rumbling boom and then everything began to shake. She'd never been in an earthquake before. "I didn't get alarmed until Mary yelled, 'It's an earthquake! Get outside!'"

The quake was a magnitude 6.4 trembler and caused brick structures to collapse across the Southland, especially in Long Beach and Compton. The quake killed 120 people; 500 more were injured.

While staying with the Nunns, Bill and Isabel slept on a Murphy Bed that slid out of the wall. "The aftershocks kept our bed going back and forth most of the night!"

Upon returning to the light station, they learned the quake had been felt at Conception too, 120 miles north. The quake had shaken the mantle off the lamp in the light tower. The men had to replace it before the lamp could be lit that evening. Several bricks were knocked out of the family's chimney which had to be repaired before a fire could be built again.

They also learned Captain Rhodes had made an inspection at Point Conception while the family was away. "We were told he had no complaints about our house," Isabel said, "but I'm sure it wasn't as clean as the houses where there weren't any children living."

She and Bill had reason to be wary of Rhodes. "Since Bill had gone over his head to get the job, I wouldn't have been surprised if he'd have made things tough for us. But there was never any sign of it."

Meanwhile, Isabel's pregnancy advanced as she hoped. She initially wanted to deliver the baby at home but soon realized the doctor was too far away to come to the light station. During a subsequent check-up—in the days when a stethoscope was considered advanced technology—the physician told Isabel, "There's going be one mighty big one or there's going to be two," and she had better come to the hospital.

Isabel went to Lompoc. One week later, on July 22, 1933, twins Jean and Joan were born, weighing 7 lbs. and 8 lbs., respectively.

But there was only one crib waiting for them at home. The parents tried keeping them in the same crib at first, but that didn't work. Bill went to town and bought another crib. Even the infants needed their space.

———

At Conception, the light tower stood 133 feet above mean water. Thick protective windows surrounded the lantern room. Two large rooms sat below, adjoining the base of the tower. A fireplace anchored the north room. The other room housed a bookshelf, a clock, and a telephone system—sometimes referred to as a "call bell"—that provided intercommunication to the dwellings and fog signal.

The lantern room housed the first-order Fresnel lens. It had been shipped to the United States from France, around Cape Horn, and on to San Francisco. On October 3, 1854, it arrived off Point Conception aboard the schooner *General Pierce* and was brought ashore at the Cojo Anchorage through the surf. Workers cleaned and assembled the lens in anticipation of installation on the new tower the following year.

The spectacular optic weighed nearly three tons. It was mounted on chariot wheels that allowed the lens to smoothly rotate once every eight-minutes. A flash of light bolted out to sea every thirty seconds.

Each keeper used a stopwatch to time the revolutions of the light. Timing checks were done periodically while on-watch to make sure the lens flashed the proper characteristic.

Bill Owens and his contemporaries worked with drop-weight mechanisms. The first three assignments of his career, Point Conception, Point Sur, and Point Arena—all of which used first-order lenses—did not have electricity when Owens arrived at each. Once electricity reached the towers, powerful bulbs, a 1,500-watt lamp at Conception, and a 1,000-watts lamp at Cabrillo, replaced the oil lamps. A one-eighth horsepower motor was installed to replace the drop-weight system. Until then, a common task for the keeper on-watch was to rewind the drop weight every few hours, and rewind again before the next keeper relieved him from duty that night.

Conception's fog-signal was the other critical navigational aid operating at the station. The first fog-signal in the United States had been a cannon, installed at Boston Light in 1719. It fired when necessary to answer the signals of ships in thick weather. Bells were later introduced and were rung by hand to answer vessels, but they lacked sufficient power for use on the seacoast. Steam whistles, and then compressed air horns—the most powerful apparatus—were devised.

More than seven hundred hours of fog blanketed Conception each year, with half that total arriving from June through August. That may represent less than ten percent of the time, but when fog hits, the danger to ships escalates greatly. The fog-signal building was located at the bottom of the hill, close to the cliff's edge. The foghorn blast was produced by compressed air and sounded on a diaphone which gave a classic two-tone bellow—first an upper tone followed by a steady lower tone. Resonators, or trumpets, were placed outside the building and projected the blast seaward.

The lens and fog apparatus demanded constant attention—each maintained in dependable working condition.

While on-watch, keepers watched the light to ensure that it kept going—and at the right speed. And they watched for fog. As soon as fog was judged to be within five miles of the station, the foghorn was activated.

The Lighthouse Service was using what they called 'pre-heater coal oil.' Keepers began to light the beacon a half-hour before sunset. "You have an alcohol torch," Owens explained decades later, "and you heat it about that high and that big around [indicates with fingers], almost red-hot with that torch. Then you have a mantle above that. When you light it, you've got to keep about fifty-five or sixty pounds of pressure on the coal oil tanks so it'll force the oil up in there."

Any failure to follow the procedure properly could result in serious problems. The men had just lit the tower at sunset one day. Isabel was outside taking laundry off the clothesline. She looked up to a frightening sight.

"What's the matter with the light?" she yelled.

The men, who had been walking back up the hill, turned to see the lantern room ablaze. On the dead run, they raced down the steps and entered the tower. They shut down the oil reservoir, sprayed their way into lantern room, and quickly had the fire snuffed.

It was what keepers called a "flare-up." "The coal oil got too cool," said Bill, "and it was still shooting coal oil through there and wasn't burning. Then it all caught fire at once."

It took the four men several hours to get everything cleaned up, but they got the light lit that night.

On occasion, a malfunction could occur, such as the flare-up, or a mechanical breakdown. In the span of seconds, keepers would find themselves in a high-stress situation that required a quick fix. Always, there loomed the possibility that the welfare of ships—and the lives of those aboard—could be suddenly in their hands, which is exactly what happened one evening.

Late one night, the fog-signal abruptly quit. All was still, quiet. No wind. No waves. Just a thick fog—like a heavy blanket that had been laid across the waters and the point. When the foghorn went dead, the man on-watch quickly called the other keepers to assist. Bill jumped out of bed, threw on some clothes, and ran to the fog-signal. As they feverishly worked to repair the generator, a ship slowly approached the point.

The vessel was proceeding, cautious-but-blind, in the fog. Razor-like rocks below the fog-signal building could easily slice mortal wounds in the vessel's hull.

In the stillness, the craft was so close to the rocks the keepers could hear voices from on deck—fearful voices. "What the hell is the matter with those lighthouse guys? I'll bet they're all sound asleep!"

Just then, the keepers finished fixing the generator and fired it up. The foghorn blasted. The startled captain ordered the ship hard-to-starboard and away from catastrophe.

The appearance of fog could be gradual or sudden. But it was always alarming. The 1930s were a time of relatively simple navigational systems. The same dead-reckoning methods employed by the destroyers at the Honda were utilized aboard the coastal freighters.

On the evening of May 28, 1933, fog blanketed the passage between the mainland and the nearby Channel Islands. The steamer *J.B. Stetson* was headed south in the soupy mist, much like that which had sent the seven destroyers to doom ten years earlier. At the same moment, the lumber schooner *Chehalis* was sailing north.

As the *J.B. Stetson's* captain strained his gaze into the mist, he spotted the lights of another ship dead ahead. Looming up suddenly out of the pea-soup fog was the *Chehalis*. The *Stetson* and the *Chehalis* were on a collision course and there was no chance to avert it.

The two vessels, both about 180 feet in length, struck each other with loud and jarring blows. The *Stetson* suffered damage along her side, but no leaking was evident. She had escaped the clutches of Conception's "graveyard" and limped into port for repair at Long Beach.

The wooden *Chehalis*, however, was badly smashed near her port bow and was leaking so fast that beaching seemed necessary to keep her from sinking. Captain H. Hansen ran her aground on the hard sandy bottom of the Cojo Anchorage, the well-protected little cove just south of the tip of Point Conception.

The **Chehalis,** *damaged in a collision, is seen beached at the Cojo Anchorage just south of Point Conception Light Station. A Coast Guard vessel waiting to assist can be seen in the distance. The photo was taken by Bill Owens the morning after the accident. (Courtesy of Owens Family)*

From Long Beach, the Coast Guard dispatched a cutter and five patrol boats to the area and safely removed the twenty-one crewmen of the *Chehalis*.

That same night, another ship ran up on the rocks. A Japanese tanker, the *Nippon Maru*, ran aground exactly where the Navy ships had at the Honda. The 400-foot tanker had been enroute from Japan to San Pedro. Efforts to refloat the *Nippon Maru* over the next few months were unsuccessful and the ship was declared a total loss in July 1933.

The following morning, Owens, toting a camera, walked to the Cojo. He checked the ship's condition and took a photograph of the vessel tucked bow-first into the sandy beach. The ship was lucky. She had suffered no damage from waves; the ocean was flat as a lake. The schooner was later patched, refloated, and repaired at Long Beach.

———

Visitors at remote light stations such as Point Conception, or Point Arguello fourteen miles to the north, were rare. In the early 1900s, hobos occasionally wandered over from the train tracks a mile away in search of meals. Infrequent guests who did arrive were usually overnight company of keepers, or sometimes other lighthouse men traveling on vacation, stopping by to see a USLHS friend.

"We had a man and his wife come down to visit us from San Francisco once," Bill recalled with a smile. "It was rough weather, and we put 'em in a room right next to the bluff. I said to the woman, 'You don't walk in your sleep, do you?'"

"No."

"Well, don't do it. Don't open that door because you'll go a hundred feet straight down."

Bill said, with a hint of a smile, they reported having gotten little sleep.

The Georges welcomed a priest to the station one Friday. In the afternoon, as he prepared to leave, it began to rain. The Georges knew he couldn't make it back to Lompoc on the muddy road and invited him to stay the night. They asked Bill and Isabel to join them all for dinner.

Point Conception's first-order Fresnel lens is now displayed at the Santa Barbara Maritime Museum. Note the impressive size of the lens and pedestal in relation to the museum visitor. (Author photo)

Mrs. George now faced a dilemma. She knew Catholics were to abstain from eating meat on Fridays. All she had was a pot-roast. She cooked it up and placed it on the table.

"I'm sorry," she said to the priest. "I don't have any fish."

The priest looked at the pot-roast and smiled.

"Oh, that's alright Mrs. George. I'll just bless it and call it fish."

Visitors at the isolated stations were common folk. An interesting exception, however, was a guest who arrived at the Point Arguello Light Station nearby. On November 29, 1916, he recorded his visit in the guest registry: "Henry Steward—world walker. I walked across the United States, Canada, Europe, part of Africa, the Holy Lands, and was in London at the breaking of the Great War. My march was in the interest of peace."

Chapter Five

Rumrunning

Saturday was cleaning day for the men each week. They mopped and waxed floors, polished brass, and thoroughly cleaned the light tower, watch room, workshop, and fog signal building. The women had brass to polish, too. It was expected that all brass in every dwelling would be shining.

The women certainly had their share of work in keeping their homes to Lighthouse Service standards. In essence, they were unpaid government labor. Mrs. George left the men to their work without intrusion, Isabel noticed. "They did not appreciate having the women getting too interested in their work. It was *their* profession."

With no television and not much radio, everyone had to make their own entertainment. Bill fished many afternoons he was off duty. Mrs. George and Mrs. Lee sometimes joined him.

But with five children, the only time Isabel could take part in activities was in the evening. Their house stood a mere twenty yards from the light tower. The living room window looked directly upon the light. The men could watch the beacon far easier from there than they could sitting in the watch room directly under the tower. In the evening, keepers and wives came over to play cards on Mr. George's and Bill's six-to-twelve watches.

Isabel's days were filled with caring for her growing family and home. Washing clothes became a continuous and cumbersome task. Bill had purchased a Maytag washer before he was hired by the Lighthouse Service. But it ran on electricity, and there was none on the station. To ease the laundry burden, Bill wanted to install a gasoline motor on the machine.

"Old Rhodes wouldn't stand for it," Isabel said. "And the head keeper on the station was scared to death of gasoline, too. So, I had to use a washboard."

Bill decided he had to find a solution. He wrote a letter to Captain Rhodes, took a page from the Sears and Roebuck catalogue, who sold the gas engines, and enclosed that in the letter. The engines, the ad said, were approved by the Underwriters Laboratory to be safe.

Soon, a letter arrived from Rhodes, through the head keeper, stating

In this view, the chute utilized to slide supplies down the hill can be seen, ending at the supply shed. Isabel's Maytag washer was located in the shed by the back porch. (Courtesy of Owens Family)

Point Conception featured stairs that required a challenging trek of 185 steps.

Bill could put the washing machine in "with proper precautions." He was instructed to install the machine out in the shed behind the back porch. Bill ran hot and cold water pipes out there. "The washing machine was certainly easier," said Isabel, "but I think the washboard got the clothes cleaner."

Family life on the light station found a sense of normalcy. Celebration of traditional holidays went unhampered by the isolation at Conception. Bill and Isabel were always prepared for Easter, Thanksgiving, and Christmas. Each year, they managed to get a Christmas tree to the station and down the hill to their house. They would decorate the tree and have the presents wrapped and ready by the time the children woke up. This, they accomplished in secrecy—or so they believed.

"I saw them one Christmas Eve when they thought I was asleep," said oldest daughter Shirley.

The Prohibition Era began on January 17, 1920. The 18th amendment to the United States Constitution banned the sale of alcohol in the United States. Canada and Mexico had no such restrictions and almost immediately the illegal transportation of alcohol across the borders of America began. Over 1,500 federal agents were tasked with enforcing the new law.

Excellent conditions existed for smugglers to get booze from the two countries into the U.S. With the Channel Islands sprinkled along the coast from Orange County to Santa Barbara County, rumrunners had virtually deserted offshore islands from which to operate—pockmarked with isolated coves and caves.

Men in the Lighthouse Service were in an awkward—if not danger-ous—position. By nature, the coastal keepers were living and working in isolated locations. What's more, they were up "at all hours" and there-fore often saw activities that were intended to go unobserved.

"Down at Conception, rum boats used to come in down at the Cojo," Bill remembered. "And trucks would come up from Los Angeles and load up with whiskey and go back to L.A. during the night. The head keeper told me, 'Don't go over there.'"

No direct pressure from bootleggers was reported by Owens. But Isabel recalled overhearing the lighthouse men discussing rum deliveries at the Cojo. They had been informed when to have the gate unlocked and to stay out of sight. The keepers never considered reporting the ille-gal activities to any authorities. "They knew what would happen if they

Bill remembered that rumrunner boats, some similar to this one, were "fast."

did," said Isabel.

The typical bootlegging process was for a fleet of "mother ships" to anchor miles off the coast—beyond the legal twelve-mile limit—in locations from Ensenada to the Channel Islands. From there, smaller vessels would ferry the illegal cargo to isolated coves and beaches. Once ashore, the bootlegging syndicates could truck the liquor to Los Angeles in less than two hours.

The profits were enormous. A twelve-bottle case of scotch sold at the ship for $50 would bring $25 a quart by the time it reached the city—a 300 percent profit.

"And the rumrunners had fast boats," Owens said.

Smuggler's boats, propelled by powerful war-surplus airplane engines, simply outran authorities. But the Coast Guard, initially underpowered, began to acquire some fast boats of its own. The government transferred several fast cutters, armed with cannons, to Southern California.

The most famous rumrunner off the coast of Santa Barbara was the quick and elusive *Grey Ghost*, a ship that possessed speed the older Coast Guard ships couldn't possibly match. Pursuits of the *Ghost* ended in frustration as she vanished with her cargo into the night. But that changed with the arrival of the fast, and armed, cutters.

One morning, the Coast Guard tailed them off the Santa Barbara Channel—on the seaward side of Santa Cruz Island. The captain of the patrol boat hollered through a loudspeaker to halt. When there was no response, they fired a warning shot in front of *Ghost's* bow. The smugglers just put on more speed. The Coast Guard eventually fired fifty-nine shells at the *Grey Ghost* after the ship failed to heave-to. Six bursts struck the ship—including one through her pilothouse.

The *Ghost* was disabled. The pilot ran her ashore on a rocky beach near Valley Anchorage on the island, then jumped over the railing and escaped. He managed to avoid two small search parties, but a third found him hiding between boulders. He was arrested. Near the wreck, floating in the water were two oak half-barrels (about twenty gallons each) of liquor. Aboard the *Ghost*, the Coast Guard discovered fifty sacks of whiskey. Sacks were packages holding six bottles jacketed in straw, three on the bottom, then two, then one, all tightly sewn in burlap.

Only the repeal of Prohibition in 1933 brought an end to the lucrative trade and the thirteen-year war against the rumrunners.

<hr />

Strong winds, Owens knew, were a constant factor along the California Coast—an aspect of nature one could do little about other than learn how to co-exist with them. Here, on the Santa Barbara Channel, the juxtaposition of land, sea, and atmospheric conditions conspired to produce sudden, strong, and sometimes dangerous gales.

"There are these mountains," Bill explained, "all along the coast down there except for this little place called Gaviota Pass. It was a bit south of the light station—between Conception and Santa Barbara. It can be calm, but the wind comes up quick down there. It starts blowing through that pass and accelerates on out to sea."

These quick changes in wind speed and temperatures were never more evident than when a "simoom"—a hot, violent wind—struck the town of Santa Barbara in 1859. Wrote George Davidson of the U.S.

The narrow mountain gap at Gaviota Pass, just south of Point Conception, often funneled hot winds out to sea that could mean trouble for mariners and extra diligence for light keepers.

Coast and Geodetic Survey Team—and discoverer of the Davidson Current—in the *Pacific Coast Pilot* thirty years later:

> The only instance of the simoom on this coast, mentioned either in its history or traditions," wrote Davidson, "was that occurring at Santa Barbara on June 17, 1859. The temperature during the morning was between 75 and 80 degrees, and gradually and regularly increased until about one o'clock P.M. when a blast of hot air from the northwest swept suddenly over the town and struck the inhabitants with terror.
>
> It was quickly followed by others. At two o'clock, the thermometer exposed to the air rose to 133 degrees and continued at or near that point for nearly three hours, whilst the burning wind raised dense clouds of impalpable dust. No human being could withstand the heat. All betook themselves to their dwellings and carefully closed every door and window. The thick adobe walls would have required days to become warmed and were consequently an admirable protection. Calves, rabbits, birds, etc., were killed; trees were blighted; fruit was blasted and fell to the ground, burned only on one side, and gardens were ruined. At five o'clock, the thermometer fell to 122 degrees, and at seven [o'clock] it stood at 77 degrees. A fisherman, in the channel in an open boat, came back with his arms badly blistered.

Davidson also reported that in the summer of 1850, near Point Conception, while engaging in astronomical observations, "we frequently experienced at night hot blasts [of wind] coming down from the Sierra Concepcion, apparently bringing the heated air from the valleys behind the Sierras. It had, of course, not near so elevated a temperature as that sweeping over Santa Barbara yet was quite fitful."

At the time Davidson was conducting observations, the western coast of the United States remained tremendously isolated from the country's eastern half. Vast prairies, deserts, and wilderness separated California from Omaha, Nebraska, and everything in between.

The transcontinental railroad was built to link the two halves. Construction began in Omaha and Oakland during the Civil War—crews laying rail in the east and west and working toward a meeting of the two. The rail link was completed in 1869 with the driving of the "Last Spike" at Promontory Summit, Utah. The Pacific Coast terminus was the Oakland Long Wharf on San Francisco Bay.

Still, no north-south rail link existed in California.

Near the turn of the 20th Century, the Southern Pacific Railroad began building such a line—from San Francisco south to Los Angeles. "The Coast Line" officially opened March 31, 1901. Tracks passed through Lompoc and within a mile of Point Conception Light Station. Southern Pacific built the small depot at Concepcion. The train was the mail link for the sparsely populated region, picking up and dropping mail posts at the depot.

Not long after Bill arrived at the light station, Concepcion's postmaster retired. Bill applied for the job and became the new postmaster. The job took very little time to perform, and no one else lived near enough to do it. When the train depot was closed by Southern Pacific in 1933, Bill moved the post office over to the light station.

Mail exchanges happened on-the-fly. As the train approached, a clerk prepared the "catcher arm," which would snatch the incoming leather mailbag Bill had hanged from a pole. The clerk would then toss the outgoing mailbag from the railcar.

The mail-drop happened once a day, near noon. Bill would be waiting when the mail pouch was thrown from the train. He sifted through the posts and delivered mail to the ranch crew. The remainder he brought back to the light.

A small shed on the light station property was turned over to Bill for the post office. His fellow keepers picked up their mail at the shed. "It was a very small community," said Isabel, "and being postmaster didn't interfere with Bill's lighthouse duties at all. But it did add to our income. Five dollars a month."

Since their early days at Conception, acquiring milk for the children was an issue. The nearest fresh milk was twenty-eight miles away. None of the keepers kept a cow on the station. None of them had children. But Isabel had young daughters who needed the calcium and vitamin D.

The Georges had previously tried to buy milk from the Cojo Ranch,

Sarah, Dixie, and Shirley are playing behind the Owens dwelling. Abalone were plentiful at the point. An intercom system connected each home with the light tower and fog-signal. The "call bell" wires are visible. (Courtesy of Owens Family)

but the foreman refused to sell. Bill spoke to the Georges about it, but Mrs. George warned him, "There's no use in asking them; they won't be bothered." In Bill's mind, that was that.

Later, however, family friends from San Francisco came to visit. Isabel cleverly asked the wife to speak with Bill about it. Soon after, Bill went to the ranch and asked for milk for the children. The Cojo folks agreed to sell. "So, we had fresh milk for the children," said Isabel. "And after the twins were born, the ranchers refused to take any money for the milk."

Early in the century, parents at Point Conception faced a problem when their children reached "school age." There was no school to attend. Children were sent to Lompoc to board with families for the school months. Though the boarding parents and families were welcoming homes, the separations were difficult for everyone. Children and their lighthouse parents looked forward to the Christmas holidays and summer.

By 1934, the Owens daughters, Shirley and Sarah, were turning seven and six, respectively. Bill and Isabel knew their priority must now be to request a transfer to a "school station" where the girls could attend.

Bill drove to the school in Lompoc and returned with the first-grade reader. Isabel took it from there. She would have Shirley sit at the table with a book in front of her while Isabel ironed clothes behind her. Looking over her daughter's shoulder, she'd call out the letter sounds and blends. Gradually, sounds and words began to make sense for Shirley. Before long, she'd completed the reader. With that success, Isabel taught Sarah to read the same way.

But the instructional limitations were significant. The girls needed to be in school.

In 1934, Bill was offered a transfer to Point Arguello Light Station where a school was nearby. But Arguello had excessive amounts of fog, which exacerbated Shirley's asthma. Bill declined the transfer. The Lighthouse Service then offered Point Reyes Light Station, about thirty miles north of San Francisco. And although a school was near enough, the station did not allow pets.

"Bill wasn't about to part with our collie," said Isabel.

The Owens girls in front of the George house at Point Conception. (Courtesy of Owens family)

In the meantime, Mr. Lee, the first assistant at Conception, had retired and Bill was made second assistant—a five dollar raise over his salary of ninety-five dollars per month.

In late January 1935, Bill received a notification his request for transfer to a school station was in process. It would require Bill to take a third-assistant position that was available. But it would be at the same pay rate as his second assistant position.

> You are advised that you have been recommended for transfer to the position of Third Assistant Keeper at Point Sur Light Station with the compensation at the rate of $1260.00 per annum effective at a date later to be reported. Upon receipt of Department authority for this transfer, you will be further advised."

[Signed] For and in the absence of the Superintendent,

O.L. Jenkins

Bill accepted the transfer.

In little more than a month, the family began preparing for their first move within the lighthouse community. For Bill, there was a mild sense of melancholy. Conception had been his first station. He'd enjoyed the friendships of his fellow keepers and, skill-wise, had prospered under the leadership of Mr. George. In his off hours, the fishing off the point was good. Owens always recalled Conception fondly as "a good station."

The girls would remember little of the years there. They were too young for many memories to take root. But they knew the family had been happy there. Isabel, it seemed, had adjusted to the unique challenges of lighthouse life. More would lay ahead at Point Sur, but she was confident they would deal with each that surfaced. Bill, she knew, was in his element on a light station.

It was Monday morning, March 11, 1935, and time to say goodbye to Conception. The family made their last climb up the long stairway. The older girls scampered up the wooden steps while Bill and Isabel carried the twins. Bill paused and looked one final time at the lantern room. The light had already been shut down that morning. Once atop the hill, the couple stopped and caught their breath. The updraft of the salty morning breeze washed over them as it had so many mornings—a pleasant memory they would often recall. The couple finished packing the car and bid goodbye to the keepers—their friends—who had gathered to wish them well.

What had been a solitary time at Conception had been a fruitful period, nonetheless. Bill had learned the necessary skills of light keeping. Isabel had delivered healthy twins and grown accustomed to the work and life on a light station. Further, she found she was well suited for it, which would prove to be providential given what lay ahead.

An unhappy Jean Owens stands with her sisters in front of the Point Sur light. Dixie, Shirley, and Sarah are behind while Jean's twin, Joan, places a comforting hand on her shoulder. Circa 1936. (Courtesy of Owens Family)

Part III

Chapter Six

Where The Wind Blows

For the second time in four years, the Owens family was making a major life change. They were headed to a school station. Their new location, at Point Sur, twenty-two miles south of Monterey, would present altogether different challenges. The couple knew they were transferring to another remote setting, one with a small nest of dwellings perched atop a wind-blown rounded mount. (The Spanish called the rock a "moro.") But the children could attend school, and that's what mattered most.

March 1935 was a troubled time across the globe. In the United States, the worst drought in American history—labeled the "Dust Bowl"—continued to engulf the interior of the country, affecting twenty-seven states. That month, Congress presented the Emergency Relief Appropriation Act to President Roosevelt, providing $525 million for drought relief.

Across the Atlantic, sinister events were developing. In Germany, Adolph Hitler formally denounced the disarmament clauses of the

Treaty of Versailles. Jews were banned from working in manual trades. And seven-hundred Christian pastors who had criticized the Nazis' state church regime were arrested.

Meanwhile, in California, the Owens family made their way north. The coast road through Big Sur, from San Simeon to Carmel, was yet to be completed; work would not be finished until 1937. That necessitated Bill driving north to Salinas before heading west on a narrow ribbon of road to Monterey. From there, they drove south, past the Hatton Ranch on the outskirts of Carmel and beyond.

They were barely past the Carmel Highlands when they could see a huge rock in the blue distance that looked like an island. It was Point Sur, rising to a height of 362 feet. Fifteen miles later, they reached the entry gate, aside the highway, to the lighthouse reservation.

From the gate, the rock sat one mile to the west—with half of the moro bordered by the ocean. The road passed through fields of thistles and dune grass until it reached a section—about 100 feet in length—of deep sand. Here was a "corduroy road" of wood planks laced together with wire. At the foot of the rock a sign advised visitors to park at the base and walk up the hill.

The profound isolation atop Point Sur is evident in this photo. The light tower is visible to the right. The keepers quarters were located on the upper left portion of the rock.

But, of course, the Owens family were to be residents, not visitors. Bill drove past the sign and began the tight-rope narrow climb to the top. "At nearly every point," one visitor to the station testified tongue-in-cheek, "[the road] is at least six inches wider than a car, and at no point is the grade over fifteen percent."

The wind, as would be the case nearly every day, whipped hard. The road of dirt and gravel eventually split in a "Y" with the left fork leading to the lighthouse itself. But the other continued to the north edge of the hill where it horseshoed right, and then turned south for a hundred yards. Soon, the family found themselves alongside a large, white-washed three-story stone house. Just beyond was the two-story home of the head keeper.

Thomas Henderson, in charge at Point Sur for three years, met Bill with a handshake and invited the family into his home. Later, he walked them around the corner and pointed to the now-vacant section of the stone triplex at the far end that would be their home. It was easily the smallest of the three keepers' quarters. But Bill was third assistant—and at the bottom rung.

The point the Owens family would live atop had first been mentioned in the logs of explorer Juan Rodriquez Cabrillo in 1552. Point Sur was not among the nominees for a lighthouse in the initial wave of construction in the 1850s. But by the early 1870s, the Lighthouse Board had made strong efforts to convince Congress of the importance of a lighthouse at that spot. Requests for construction funds were made—and each year they were refused. Finally, in 1886, Congress agreed to fund the project.

It's a testament to the tenacity of the United States Lighthouse Service that the station could be built at all. The hill was a forbidding and lifeless setting. One survivor of the SS *Los Angeles*—shipwrecked there in 1873—declared, "God Almighty never made a worse possible place for a wreck than this same Point Sur."

Originally, the rock had only ten or twelve feet of flat ground at its peak and no appreciable amount of soil. The top would have to be blasted level to provide space for the necessary buildings. And blast away the government did. Atop the hill, the sites for the lighthouse, triplex, engine house, and cistern were blown from the rock with dynamite. A pump and pumphouse were built at the base of the moro and pipes laid to transfer water from a mountain spring to the cistern above.

Workers dynamited ocean-side portions of the hill to construct a road of dirt and gravel from the base to the summit, including the fork to the northwestern edge of the rock where the lighthouse was to be built. When the work was done, the brutally difficult engineering and construction project had been accomplished—in just two years.

The lighthouse engineers had built a sturdy gray-stone light tower and fog-signal at the north end. The tower itself was thirty-eight-feet tall. Because of space limitations on the rock, the lantern room and fog-signal room were included in the tower. The oil house was constructed just south of the lighthouse.

Supplies delivered by tenders were lifted by a steam hoist to the wharf seen here. The tramway is visible ascending the steep hill.

The lens was a first-order Fresnel, built in Paris in the year 1887. The brilliant collection of prisms contained sixteen panels, was mounted on an iron pedestal, and rotated on chariot wheels. On August 1, 1889, the lantern was lit for the first time. The beam of light was visible an astounding twenty-three miles out to sea.

The light itself stood 270-feet above water in perhaps the windiest spot on an already wind-beaten point. Keepers braced themselves whenever they left the lantern room. Men grabbed the railings along the balustrade and the metal handholds attached to the iron window frames. Rare was the day when a keeper needn't hold his hat down to retain possession.

In the early days of the light station, getting supplies down the existing coast road from Monterey was a dangerous venture. More a stage trail, it was winding, narrow, strewn with rocks, and bordered by steep drop-offs on the ocean side.

Until the mid-1930s, lighthouse tenders were the station's primary means of resupply and relief. The ships brought supplies to Point Sur every four months, including food, coal, gasoline, and kerosene, as well as paints, polishes, and cleaning supplies.

"Of course, if there were any roads," Owens said, "they'd truck in supplies. But [with] remote or offshore stations everything was brought in by boat."

Tenders anchored off the southeastern end of the moro, then launched surfboats, or "skiffs," filled with goods.

Lighthouse engineers had built a wharf at the foot of the hill about forty or fifty feet in height. Goods were ferried from the tender to the foot of the wharf and placed atop the landing by a steam hoist.

Cargo was then placed and secured in a rail cart. The "supply car" was raised or lowered by cable, a trip of 280 feet via a steep tramway. The system was powered by a donkey engine.

Tenders would bring gasoline for the generators in drums. After being hauled to the top, the fuel was then transferred by gravity through pipes to the oil house. As the drums were emptied, keepers stored them down on the wharf. When the next tender arrived months later, the men simply rolled the drums off the wharf into the ocean where the skiffs would retrieve them.

The south cove had been selected by the Lighthouse Service as the landing site because it was the best protected option. The surf, from most swell directions, was far reduced compared to waves breaking elsewhere around the rock. But the capricious Pacific could never be fully trusted and rogue waves sometimes appeared from nowhere.

Goods were pulled up to the top by rail car. (Courtesy of Point Sur Light Keepers)

The tender *Lupine* was sailing south on November 23, 1933, delivering needed supplies to coastal light stations. That morning, a boat crew of four men had just discharged a load of provisions at the wharf and were returning to the vessel in their supply boat. It was early, 8 A.M., and the small craft jostled uneasily as she headed to the *Lupine*.

Suddenly, a monstrous wave wrapped around the point and swept toward the *Lupine*. Lightkeepers atop the wharf yelled a warning but were helpless to assist. The crew aboard the tender watched the huge swell lift the *Lupine* as it surged past. The four men and their skiff disappeared from the *Lupine's* sight below the rising wall of water.

Keepers, newspaper reporters later wrote, stared in horror from atop the wharf. As the rogue wave broke, whitewater rolled and exploded skyward like a geyser. When the roiling surf finally began to simmer, two men bobbed to the surface, struggling to cling to the overturned boat. A rescue launch from the *Lupine* arrived to pull the pair out of the sea. But two other crew members were missing. Wilhelm Kiahn and Jens Haagerson had been swept under by the turbulence.

Their bodies washed up on the beach the following day.

The *Pacific Grove Tribune* wrote, "Lightkeepers said that supplies were commonly landed when surf was running higher than was the case the day of the drownings. But they had never seen a mountainous swell

The lighthouse tender **Lupine.** *(Courtesy of Point Sur Light Keepers)*

appear without warning."

———————

Now in Spring 1935, the Owens family walked with Tom Henderson, who had witnessed the Lupine tragedy, back to the head keeper's home. Henderson explained, somewhat apologetically, that the Owens would have tighter quarters than expected.

The week before, Henderson had received a copy of a letter from Captain Rhodes alerting him of the family's need for "living space." Rhodes knew that with five children they would benefit from as much room as could be made available. The letter had been addressed to the second assistant keeper, Mr. Harmon Day, and cc'd to Tom Henderson and Bill Owens.

It read:

> In reply to an inquiry by this Office on November 30th, the Keeper of your station advised that the garret room on the third floor of your quarters was not occupied by you. You are therefore directed to turn this room over in a clean condition to the new Third Assistant

Keeper, Mr. William Owens, who will report for duty on or about March 11th.

[Signed]
H.W. Rhodes

After the second assistant received the letter, circumstances in the garret quickly changed. The Day family, which hadn't used the room until they received orders to turn it over, moved their high-school aged child into the garret. Now, head keeper Henderson informed Bill and Isabel the room was occupied.

At the time, the couple didn't know what a bad piece of news that would be.

The whitewashed stone building housed all three assistant keepers. Harry Miller was the first assistant and Harmon Day the second. Their quarters had plenty of space. The Owens family moved into the cramped third keeper's home. From the start, the quarters presented significant logistical challenges for the family of seven.

Chief among them was the bathroom—located on the third floor. There were always two flights of stairs to climb to reach the toilet. With five wait-'til-the-last-minute children, particularly the twins who were two years old, plenty of accidents occurred before they could get to the third floor. No logical alternative could be found for a commode. Downstairs was the kitchen, living room, and pantry—none of which would work. And they couldn't place it in the hallway since the second assistant's family shared that passageway.

After several discussions, Bill and Isabel decided the three youngest would share a second-floor bedroom, with Dixie in a single bed and the twins in two cribs. Bill and Isabel would use the other bedroom on the floor—so small it barely held their double bed and a chest of drawers. The couple thought the twins were too young to sleep any further away from them. On the third floor, along with the bathroom, a small bedroom was assigned to Shirley and Sarah.

The bedrooms were lilliputian; the only way for Isabel to clean the floors was to crawl under the beds and sweep with a hand-brush. New behaviors had to be learned: stopping to allow another to pass, avoiding a child quickly rounding a corner, turning sideways to create space. The sheer frustration of life within a sardine can suddenly was a daily reality. Though no one was claustrophobic, one couldn't have blamed them if they became so.

North of the triplex was a water tower; its purpose was to provide water pressure for the flush toilets that had been installed on the third floor of each triplex unit. The pipes from the kitchen and bathroom merged below the dwellings and carried the contents by gravity several hundred feet westward to be discharged into the ocean. In 1935, there were no other options.

Despite the difficult living conditions atop Point Sur, Bill and Isabel recognized the original lighthouse engineers had done everything possible to make the rock livable. Soil had been imported so that each family could grow flowers and vegetables. But the rocky hilltop presented severe limitations that even the engineers couldn't fully assuage.

To the north of the triplex and tower stood a barn with a wooden platform to enable keepers to have a cow if they desired—which the Henderson family did. The cow's name was "Beauty." The railing of the platform was intended to protect her from the steep drop-off down the bluff. The cow provided enough milk for everyone on the station.

The "primitive" conditions on the light station applied to more than just the plumbing. The only heating source for the keeper's dwellings was coal. There were no electric lights; families used lamps and lanterns. Nor was there garbage service to Point Sur.

The flies were terrible atop the hill. None of the assistant's quarters had screen doors—and Henderson wouldn't order one. Isabel tried spraying, but with no visible benefit. The next day there'd be just as many of the irritating insects.

"We threw all our trash down the hill behind the house," she said. "Everybody did it. And *that's* where all the flies came from."

The sheer beauty of the Big Sur region provided little relief from the constraints of the light station. Bill was continually busy with his work and there was rarely a chance to leave the rock-strewn summit. Big Sur's steep mountains and narrow canyons—so close by—served only to remind them how their lodgings felt like a corset too-tightly strapped

The Henderson's cow, "Beauty," enjoying the deck outside the barn. From left are Dixie, unidentified family friend, Sarah, and Shirley. (Courtesy of Point Arena Light Keepers)

around their torso.

Nevertheless, Bill's experience operating the lens at Conception had prepared him well for Point Sur. Both locations were major navigational points along the California coast, and both were equipped with first-order Fresnel lenses. Sur was home to a massive optic standing an impressive nine feet nine inches in height.

"Point Sur's lens ran on chariot wheels," Owens said. "If you kept the dust off the chariot wheels and the rails then they ran fine. You had to grease the wheels once in a while. But sometimes that dust would build up and stop the light from turning."

The station used an incandescent oil vapor lamp that functioned like Coleman lanterns used by campers. Oil was pumped from a reservoir, converted into a gas, then drawn up to the mantle. There, the gas ignited and produced a bright, glowing white light. The mantles were eight inches in length and lasted about a week. Keepers trimmed them before the lamp was lit each night.

The Fresnel lens at Point Sur contained sixteen panels—each with a bullseye center—and so efficiently collected and magnified the light

Isabel and Bill pose with Shirley, Dixie, and Sarah, in front of keeper's triplex at Point Sur circa 1936. (Courtesy of Owens Family)

source that it produced a one-million candlepower beam. The light displayed one flash every fifteen seconds. Keepers climbed a short spiral stairway to reach the lantern room.

Walking to the light tower in the dark, keepers were exposed and vulnerable. Howling winds were the norm and maintaining one's balance took full concentration. In the darkness of late-evening watches, every step the keeper took was measured—and made with exceptional care.

"Worst station I was ever on," Bill said. "The wind got so bad you couldn't get down to the lens. Had to fight your way down there."

At no other station did Bill worry about his safety. But he felt differently about this place. "You had to be careful at Point Sur," said the keeper. "You had to hang onto something or you could get blown off the tower."

A unknown keeper walks the gallery outside the first-order lens. Note the handles in the iron window frames. In howling winds, keepers clung to these to prevent being blown off the tower.

Chapter Seven

The Macon

J ust a month before the Owens family arrived, the wind at
Point Sur had made history, triggering the most noteworthy disaster
in Point Sur history—the wreck of the USS *Macon*. She was a rigid dirigible and a star of the Navy's Lighter Than Air fleet. The 785-foot silver
airship, nearly as large as Germany's famed *Hindenburg*, came to grief on
February 12, 1935, and was front-page headlines in virtually every newspaper across the nation.

It was a wind-related tragedy, rooted in a history marred by dirigible
accidents. For several decades, the United States Navy had experimented
with the military usefulness of such airships. It was believed they could
fill a valuable role in scouting enemy troop and fleet movements from
the sky. The Navy began its Lighter Than Air, or LTA, program in 1915
and spent millions to construct a series of dirigibles, the USS *Los Angeles, Shenandoah, Akron*, and *Macon*. The first airships were launched in
the early 1920s.

But the program was plagued by disaster. The USS *Shenandoah* was the first to succumb. During a flight in 1925, the ship was caught in severe weather and broke apart over Ohio. Out of a crew of forty men, fourteen were killed in the accident.

Undeterred, the Navy continued to pursue the project. The USS *Akron*, launched in 1931, was regarded as a potential "flying aircraft carrier." Within her hull was a compliment of Sparrowhawk biplane fighters. The planes were launched and retrieved by a "trapeze" hook installation on the underbelly of the dirigible.

But the *Akron* was struck down on the evening of April 3, 1933, while she was participating in exercises over the Atlantic Coast. Aboard the flight were two names of note: Rear Adm. William Moffett, instrumental in the development of naval aviation, and Lt. Comdr. Herbert Wiley, who would later command the *Macon*.

The *Akron* encountered fog not long after she left the mooring mast at Lakehurst, New Jersey, where, four years later, the *Hindenburg* would explode, killing thirty-five. That night, the *Akron* was battered by the strong winds and turbulence of a storm front. Shortly after midnight, the airship crashed into the Atlantic off the New Jersey coast. No life jackets were aboard the *Akron*. The accident killed seventy-three men, including Rear Admiral Moffett. Only three crew members survived, among them Wiley.

Still, the Navy held out hope for the future of the dirigible program. An opportunity to demonstrate the airship's usefulness arose in June 1934. President Franklin Roosevelt was returning from a trip to Hawaii aboard the heavy cruiser USS *Houston*. The newly promoted Commander Wiley and the crew of the USS *Macon* located the *Houston* amid the Pacific, and, using the Sparrowhawks, dropped copies of current newspapers on the cruiser's deck for the Commander-in-Chief.

The mission surprised both the president and the captain of the *Houston*. A message from the cruiser was sent to the *Macon*: "The President compliments you and your planes on your fine performance and excellent navigation." Later, the airship received a second message: "Well done and thank you for the newspapers. The President."

Now, in the winter of 1935, the *Macon* was flying enroute from San

Diego to Moffett Field in Sunnyvale, named for the admiral who had perished aboard the Akron just two years before. It was late Tuesday afternoon.

The Navy's light cruisers were on exercise maneuvers. The *Macon* had been serving as scout for the vessels. Point Sur lighthouse keepers watched in awe as the massive silver airship flew gracefully above the ships of the Pacific Fleet.

The fleet was headed north, abreast of Point Sur. The *Macon* was elegantly cruising through the skies, her giant frame outlined above a low fog.

Then, something went terribly wrong. A sudden squall battered the airship. A wind shear ripped away her upper tailfin. Gas cells near the aft end were punctured, causing the craft to plunge toward the ocean just off Point Sur. Crew members clutched the nearest stable object to keep from falling as the airship lurched in every direction.

Faced with sudden and catastrophic damage, Commander Wiley barked a series of rapid orders. Ballast was dropped to slow the fall of the airship. But with the quick purge of weight, the *Macon* began an out-of-control climb to an altitude of 4,850 feet. Wiley flashed the first

The giant USS Macon *seen flying over New York City in the summer of 1933.*

S.O.S. at 5:15 P.M. and called for immediate assistance. To regain altitude control, he ordered helium to be vented. The massive airship began a descent to the water.

Navy vessels, above which the *Macon* had been flying, had already thrown over their rudders to steer toward the anticipated crash site. The final S.O.S. from Wiley read, "Will abandon ship as soon as we land on the water."

For a time, the dirigible disappeared into the fog. It took nearly twenty minutes for the mortally wounded *Macon* to gradually descend to the sea. She settled gently on the surface and slowly began to sink. The crew, which had been dispersed throughout the hull of the airship, abandoned the Macon as soon as she struck the water, wearing life preservers and clinging to floats. As dusk turned to dark, searchlight beams from the cruisers scanned the waters for survivors. Navy rescue lifeboats surged about in the light swells, then stopped to pluck desperate sailors from the sea.

Out of a crew of eighty-three men, all but two survived. One jumped from the airship high above the water and was killed at impact. Officers believed the other victim, a mess attendant, was overcome by the helium before he could escape.

The sensational story dominated the news headlines. Even the Lindbergh baby kidnapping verdict, announced the same day, was relegated to single column print in the shadows of the *Macon* story.

Almost immediately, the United States Navy conducted a Board of Inquiry. It took place aboard the USS *Tennessee* in San Francisco Bay on Feb 16, 1935. Testimony from the *Macon's* officers was presented. The court also heard eye-witness accounts from the Point Sur lighthouse keepers.

"It happened at one time and reminded me of a paper sack exploding," testified assistant keeper, Harry Miller.

Mr. Henderson testified "the *Macon* was about three miles offshore. I was watching it through glasses. When it was just about abreast of the point, the fin seemed to go to pieces very suddenly. The fabric drifted back. Some of it caught on the rudder."

"The fin tore loose at one place. Then, there was a pause, then more tearing until the entire fin appeared naked. I could see a hole in the top of the hull."

Miller noted that the ship dipped slightly, then bore left toward the sea. "She seemed to start gaining elevation then but continued to make a circle and headed back south and disappeared among the clouds."

Even after the *Macon* was concealed by clouds and fog, the keepers were able to follow her course by seeing the large splashes of objects falling into the water. (Ballast was thrown overboard in a futile effort to keep the craft aloft.)

The death plunge of radio man Ernest Dailey was described to the board of inquiry by an eyewitness, Rudderman W.H. Clarke. As the airship wallowed in the sky, said Clarke, "I met Dailey in the port keel and went up to get clear of the ship. We talked about the advisability of leav-

The February 12, 1935, edition of the Monterey Peninsula Herald *reported the news of the* Macon's *sinking. (Author photo)*

ing the ship. I told Dailey it was [still] too far to jump. Without warning, he jumped, feet first, turned over slowly several times and I didn't see him anymore. He jumped at approximately 175 feet."

The wreck of the *Macon* brought the Lighter Than Air program to an abrupt end.

The crash and sinking "was all anybody talked about at the light station for weeks," Isabel said.

On March 1, the *Oakland Tribune* wrote an anecdote to the historic event. Henderson, Point Sur's head keeper, "was probably one of the last men to see from the ground the *Macon* as it plunged into its watery grave. Yet, when newspapermen [later] rushed to the lighthouse, he was not around."

"He's busy," Henderson's wife, Verna, told the reporters.

"Doesn't he know that the *Macon* has fallen?" one asked.

"Sure, but he's busy," his wife replied. "He's out milking!"

The *Tribune* story read humorously enough. It also illustrated Mrs. Henderson's tendency to give orders—an inclination of hers that would one day nudge Bill Owens to the verge of resigning from the Lighthouse Service.

———

The handful of children at the light station had only recently been able to attend school in a classroom. Earlier, the county had provided a teacher on the station who would live with the head keeper's family. Classes were held in a shed behind the dwelling.

In the early 1930s, the federal government built a one-room schoolhouse on the lighthouse reservation. It was located on a small flat near the entry gate. "I remember the fields around the school were covered with thistles," said Shirley, an Owens daughter who was seven when the family moved to Point Sur.

Teachers at remote light stations were typically new college graduates—and female. The county paid the teacher's salary. Young educators were willing to tolerate the isolated conditions, if only for a short period, to acquire "classroom" experience.

Miss June Gilbert was exactly that. She was a recent college graduate and a resident of Pacific Grove, about twenty miles north. Gilbert was the teacher at the new Lighthouse School when the Owens girls moved to Point Sur. When she would arrive at school each morning, she'd build a fire in the wood stove. The classroom was toasty by the time students arrived.

Nine children attended, four from the lighthouse, three girls from the nearby Grimes Ranch, and two boys from another ranch. High school-aged students attended Monterey High School, transported to town by their parents.

Shirley and six-year-old Sarah were assigned two lessons in each subject every day. Miss Gilbert's strategy worked; both girls caught up to their age peers. Bill and Isabel appreciated Gilbert's flexibility and confidence in their daughter when she allowed Dixie to attend school whenever she wanted, even though she was not yet of school age. The teacher

Bill ferried the children each day to the one-room lighthouse school located near the highway. The bordering fence can be seen on the far right. (Courtesy of Owens Family)

believed the experience would make Dixie's official school entry easier for her.

To the Owens girls, school life was a novelty. They were excited to finally be able to experience it. "Miss Gilbert gave us a lot of individual attention," said Shirley.

Bill drove the three girls down the hill to school each day; Isabel hadn't learned to drive yet. Bill was going to teach her, but after one harrowing trip up the hill, "he said I should learn somewhere else."

———

The Owens family had been at the station a year when the light's first assistant, Harry Miller, was transferred to Point Cabrillo. Second assistant Harmon Day's family moved to the Miller's vacated quarters and the Owens family was permitted to move into the Day's. Now, at last, the family had enough room. The second assistant's living space, the middle quarters, was considerably larger.

Isabel still had a first-floor living room, kitchen, and pantry. But the girls' upstairs bedroom was so large it could fit all five children's beds without the slightest feeling of being cramped.

Again, the couple chose to sleep in the other second-floor bedroom, close to the twins, who, at three-years of age, were too young for school. This left the garret room on the third floor for guests, which came in handy when the family had friends visit.

The Lighthouse Service allowed guests to visit keeper families on the station, as long as the gatherings didn't overlap with inspections or major repair work. Standard procedure required keepers to submit a written request to the District Office for permission.

Most guests stayed only a few days, but on several occasions, Bill and Isabel had friends visit for nearly two weeks. It is a safe bet that, upon leaving Point Sur, friends wondered aloud, "How do they do it?"

The Owens girls in 1936 on the driveway behind the triplex. Clockwise, back row, are Shirley, Sarah, Dixie, Jean, and Joan. Thomas Henderson's home is visible in the background right. (Courtesy of Owens Family)

The road from the highway to the light station wasn't paved in 1935. Wooden planks lined the stretch of dunes between the hill and the dirt portion of the road. Often, the wind would cover the boards with a heavy feathering of sand. The men would then work in teams of two to lift the boards up and place them back on top of the sand. It was a necessary task if one wanted to drive across the dunes to the school or the highway, something Bill needed to do daily.

Despite the preponderance of gales at the point, there were times when nature would deliver a breathtaking day. Isabel recalled one such occasion that was both strange and magnificent. She awoke early one morning to hear the foghorn blowing. Expecting thick fog, she was stunned to see a brilliant blue sky across the ocean. She walked outside to find the air still and quiet. Only the periodic foghorn and the distant sound of waves breaking at the rock's base could be heard. Crystal clear skies surrounded the hill in every direction. But down below, a layer of fog covered the ocean, like a bowl of clam chowder, as far as she could see.

Though they had an indoor bathroom and running water, as was the case at Conception, they did not have electricity. "We didn't have a refrigerator," said Isabel. "We used a cooler. It kept things cool, but it didn't keep them cold. We didn't have ice blocks either. The cooler was insulated. You just couldn't keep things very long."

Other inconveniences presented themselves daily, one being a place for the children to play. Almost every flat space at the top of the hill had long ago been obligated to the needs of the light station.

The girls sometimes played behind the triplex by the garage. The driveway circled the building atop the hill. The girls often climbed a large rock behind the garage, but that usually ended with one of them getting a scrape. As at Conception, wherever the children roamed, indoors or out, they were never out of the watchful eye of Shep.

In the summer months, Isabel and Mrs. Miller took the children down to the south beach. The waters to the north side of the hill were far too dangerous with large breakers crashing and sweeping up the beach. The girls loved the beach trips, during which they built sandcastles and hunted for shells. They went often, but never alone.

When nearby ranchers, the Grimes family, hosted a barn-raising dance, the Owens

Isabel and Shirley minding the laundry chores. Clothing had to be securely pinned to the line and could only be done in light breezes. (Courtesy of Owens Family)

Isabel is dressed and ready for the barn dance at the Grimes Ranch. The evening was a rare excursion away from the light station. All the Owens girls accompanied her. (Courtesy of Owens Family)

family happily accepted the invitation to attend, all except for the dance-avoidant Bill. The ranch was not far from the lighthouse and several children from the Grimes family attended class with Miss Gilbert. "I put the children down for a nap that afternoon," Isabel recalled. "But Shirley said she couldn't sleep because her feet 'felt like dancing.' None of us did much dancing, but we enjoyed the evening anyway."

While Bill's relationships with fellow assistant keepers and their wives were pleasant enough, a rift developed between him and head keeper Henderson. Each assistant keeper bought their milk from the Hendersons. The Owens family, with five children, needed plenty of it, and were daily customers. But one day, that came to a halt.

An issue came up between Bill and Mr. Henderson. "Bill never told me what it was about," said Isabel, "but afterward, Mr. Henderson decided to stop selling us milk from his cow." Bill made no effort to change Henderson's mind. Instead, he arranged for a dairy in Monterey to drop three quarts of milk off every day at the gate by the highway; he'd drive down to pick them up.

Eventually, Henderson offered to sell the family milk again, but Bill was unsettled enough by the head keeper's earlier decision that he declined the offer.

"The head keeper and I, we couldn't get along," said Bill.

That was putting it mildly. Once, according to Owens, the man was so peeved at Bill he said, "If I was your wife, I'd feed you poison."

Bill replied, "If you were my wife, I'd eat it."

Over time, the conditions at Point Sur had added to Bill's frustration. The wind was wearing him out. So was the postage-stamp-sized living space atop the rock. But what trumped both was the manner in which work directives were dispersed. A pattern had emerged where Henderson would pass instructions to the assistants through his wife.

In particular, Bill detested the head keeper's wife wielding so much power. "She'd come out and say, 'Tom wants you three fellows to paint this building.' So, I asked her, 'When the hell did you get put on payroll?'

I got in trouble."

While at Point Conception, all directives came through Mr. George—a standard that Bill was accustomed to. And, as Isabel had mentioned, the wives had stayed clear of the lighthouse operations; it was the keeper's profession, not the wives. To Bill, receiving his instructions from Verna Henderson was demeaning and disrespectful. And on a spring day in 1937, it happened once too often.

An angry Owens jumped in the car and backed it out of the garage, a spontaneous symbol of "I have had *enough*."

"Where you going?" Henderson asked.

"To the District Office."

"I didn't give you permission to go."

"I didn't ask for it either. I'm still going."

Bill drove to San Francisco, marched into the Custom House, and demanded a transfer. "I can't get along with that guy down there."

The Owens family poses in front of the garage with family friends visiting the station. (Courtesy of Owens Family)

When told they were unsure about any openings, a resolute Bill shook his head.

"Alright, I'll have to quit then."

"Don't quit," Oliver Jenkins, the Assistant Superintendent of Lighthouses, 18th District, told him. "Go back and we'll call you. We'll find something for you."

Weeks later, Jenkins called with good news: the district was transferring Owens to Point Arena, about 100 miles north of San Francisco.

Had Captain Rhodes, instead of Jenkins, been in the office that moment, the outcome might have been different. Rhodes could still have resented being "forced" to hire the keeper back in 1931. But Providence smiled on Owens that day. His complaint had been heard by a patient and understanding ear.

He received a written offer of a second assistant position at $1,200 per year, to start on or about July 1, 1937. Although the letter referred to a "second assistant" position, Owens was to be transferred as third assistant—the slot open at Point Arena. He would, however, still receive second assistant pay. It mattered little to Owens. His relief was palpable—he was leaving Point Sur.

But he had no idea of the tempest that lay just ahead—one he would not be able to avoid. Nor would Captain Rhodes.

Part IV

Chapter Eight

Coming Home

A sense of excitement, the same the family had known on their way to Point Conception six years earlier, charged the atmosphere on moving day. For Bill, it was a day of deliverance. He'd avoided any disciplinary action for leaving the station without permission; and thanks to the patience of Oliver Jenkins, Owens had "fallen up" with the transfer to Point Arena.

The family piled into their Ford sedan and headed north. Soon, Owens could see Point Sur in his rearview mirror—just where he wanted it. Anticipation mounted with each hour, especially as they reached San Francisco. The family would be crossing the new Golden Gate Bridge. The span, painted in "International Orange," had opened only two months earlier.

More than 200,000 awestruck pedestrians had crossed the bridge on foot—or roller skates—the day before vehicle traffic was allowed. Bill and Isabel had never seen anything like it as they drove midspan,

Point Arena Light Station

746-feet above the ocean. The bridge toll per car was fifty cents—a substantial sum in the Depression year of 1937.

Further north, the Coast Highway weaved left and right, rolled up and down, but was almost never straight. Finally, they reached the small town of Point Arena, population 480, twenty-eight miles south of the then-lumber town of Mendocino. Owens pulled into the gas station and asked, just as he had in Lompoc, "Where is the light station?"

"Five miles north of town," the attendant replied. "Turn left on Lighthouse Road."

It had been a long day of travel.

"First one to see the lighthouse gets a nickel!" Isabel said.

The children yelped in glee; they were almost home. A few minutes later, Shirley won the nickel.

Bill slowed to observe the "right-of-way" as cows wandered unrestricted and grazed wherever they pleased. The bluffs above the ocean, sixty feet high, surrounded the light tower on three sides. The fog-signal building was located just beyond the tower toward the point. There, reefs extended from the shoreline in all directions—like a rocky sunburst.

Owens found the gate closed but unlocked. He could see the tall

The Owens family moved into this cottage when they arrived on station in 1937. The Packard parked in front was purchased by Bill from another keeper. (Courtesy of Point Arena Light Keepers)

white cylindrical light tower in the distance—dominating the point. A few hundred yards further, they reached the four keeper's quarters on the right. Each dwelling was identical—and beautiful. The two-story wooden homes had long, sloping, red-shingled roofs and sun porches that extended the length of the house. A three-pronged red brick chimney stood atop the peak of each roof.

In front of one such cottage stood a trim gray-haired gentleman, head keeper Elmer Williams, who welcomed the family and, once Bill delivered his transfer papers, directed them to their new home. It was the fourth dwelling—the one closest to the light tower and fog-signal.

Gazing across the light station for the first time, the eyes of the Owens family widened with wonder. They knew little about Point Arena, a place that would prove as idyllic and fulfilling as the family would ever know.

The lighthouse reservation that welcomed the Owens family that day was far different from the original built in 1870. The first lighthouse had been a picturesque cylindrical brick-and-mortar tower. Adjacent to it stood a lovely Stick and Gothic Revival four-plex which housed the four light keepers and their families.

Beyond the light, toward the point, was the fog-signal building constructed of old growth redwood. Turn-of-the-century visitors to the station were awestruck by the beauty of the point of land, the splendid
views in all directions, and the stately New England-styled tower and
buildings.

The light station had been constructed by Lt. Col. R.S. Williamson
of the Army Corps of Engineers, the same engineer who had directed the
construction of the third lighthouse at Point Conception in 1881. But
unknown to all—including the skilled Williamson—the San Andreas
Fault lay just three and a half miles east of the lighthouse reservation.
The fault, California's oldest—and most tempestuous—resident, generally rested dormant for decades except for an occasional tremor or two.
But its explosive potential was ever-present and early on the morning of
April 18, 1906, its fury unleashed.

The Great San Francisco Earthquake struck at 5:12 A.M. Almost
everything that had been built near the fault was destroyed. The quake
lasted forty-five seconds. It ruptured the northernmost 296-miles of

*The original light station prior to the 1906 earthquake. The tower and fourplex were
destroyed by the quake. The fog-signal building can be seen to the left. (Courtesy of
Point Arena Light Keepers)*

the fault from San Juan Batista, eighty miles south of San Francisco, to Cape Mendocino, two-hundred miles north of the city. In San Francisco, more than 3,000 people died and the homes of more than 250,000 residents were destroyed. Libraries, art treasures, and family heirlooms were suddenly gone. Schools, churches, hospitals—gone.

In Point Arena, every brick building had been reduced to rubble in a matter of seconds. The Davey Crockett Saloon, reported the *Ukiah Dispatch*, was "leveled to the ground, not a brick left standing." The high school burned to the ground. Most of the wooden structures in town had been jarred completely off their foundations.

The shockwaves generated by the quake traveled northward at a phenomenal 8,300 miles per hour. (A jet airliner cruises at 550.) It took a mere forty seconds for the tremors that began in San Francisco to rip their way up the hills and valleys to the Point Arena Light Station ninety-five miles away.

The keeper's log-book recorded the event:

> A heavy blow first struck the tower from the south. The blow came quick and heavy, accompanied by a heavy report. The tower quivered for a few seconds, went far over to the north, came back, and then swung north again, repeating this several times. Immediately after came rapid and violent vibrations, rendering the tower apart, the sections grinding and grating upon each other; while the lens, reflector, etc., in the lantern were shaken from their settings and fell in a shower upon the floor.

The earthquake devastated the light tower. Though it did not collapse, the lighthouse was so badly damaged it had to be dismantled. The keeper's fourplex was cracked and twisted far beyond repair. But, incredibly, no one was injured on the station.

Prior to the earthquake, the lands along the San Andreas were shifting but at an imperceptible pace—one-half inch per year. On April 18, however, the land jolted and lurched sideways an astounding sixteen feet in only forty-five seconds. Geologists today estimate the disaster at 7.9 on the Richter Scale.

The movement was so violent at Point Arena that geologists originally surmised the epicenter was below the town itself. Geological studies later concluded the actual epicenter was two miles off the coast of San Francisco, just beyond the Golden Gate.

At Point Arena, a temporary tower was quickly built to provide a "light aid" to the mariner. A second-order lens was requisitioned and placed atop the makeshift thirty-foot wooden tower. The government sent building crews to the station who scaffolded the light tower to safely disassemble it. What could be salvaged was reused or repurposed. The original lighthouse iron circular stairway was saved for installation in the future tower. Rubble was simply bulldozed off the edge of the bluffs and into the ocean.

Work then began to rebuild the station and replace the equipment essential to operation of the light. Interestingly, the wooden fog-signal building survived the quake and continued to operate. The redwood "flexed" during the earthquake while bricks did not.

The USLHS decided to abandon all previous construction models and consulted with a San Francisco-based company to build the new lighthouse. This one would need to be capable of withstanding future earthquakes. The newly enlisted company specialized in building factory smokestacks featuring steel reinforcing bars encased in concrete.

A temporary light tower was built to house a second-order lens until the old tower could be removed and a new one built. The work was completed in only 14 months.

The new Point Arena lighthouse, the first steel-reinforced concrete light tower in the United States, began operation on September 18, 1908. At 115 feet in height, the tower equaled Pigeon Point Lighthouse, located north of Santa Cruz, as the tallest of all West Coast lighthouses. The lantern room displayed a brilliant new first-order Fresnel lens.

Brick-and-mortar was never used again in the construction of an American lighthouse.

———————

In the summer of 1937, former King Edward VIII of England—now the Duke of Windsor—married the American divorcee, Wallis Simpson. The Spanish Civil War was raging. Famed aviator Amelia Earhart and her navigator Fred Noonan disappeared over the Pacific Ocean—never to be found. And a forty-five-year-old professor from Oxford named John Ronald Reuel Tolkien published a story he'd written for his own children called *The Hobbit*.

Meanwhile, members of the Owens family were beginning their own new adventure. The change from the cramped, wind-blown, and isolated confines of Point Sur to the open reaches of the pastures and spacious quarters at Point Arena could hardly have been greater—or more welcome.

Isabel was delighted with the family's new living conditions. There was a fenced front yard and side yard—and a front porch that stretched the length of the house. Beyond the cottage entryway was a large living room and, to the left, a good-sized dining room. Fireplaces anchored the corners of both. Beyond the dining room was a spacious kitchen. Straight beyond the living room wall was a utility room and bathroom; and to the right were two bedrooms. Space abounded, "even for a family of seven," Isabel would later declare.

Upstairs were two more bedrooms, leaving a spare room for visitors. For the first time since joining the Lighthouse Service in 1931, the Owens family could relax in comfortable living quarters.

"The kitchen was the coziest room in the house," Shirley Owens remembered. "It had a coal stove which was going all day and night.

When one of us was sick, we'd get to sit in the Morris chair close to the stove. The cure-all was toast, warm milk, and the chair."

Behind the house was a large field, a shed for coal, and a barn. The latter had stabled horses earlier in the century but now served as storage. Eventually, the family would put a smaller sloped-roof barn to good use after the purchase of a milking cow, "Bessie."

Although the light tower and the fog-signal had electricity, the cost-conscious Lighthouse Service had not extended electrical power to the dwellings.

Jean Owens, four years old at the time the family arrived at Point Arena, would later write, "Living without electricity when I was a child didn't seem unusual. It's just the way it was. We had kerosene lanterns for light, two fireplaces, and a coal kitchen stove for warmth. For hot water, Mom had to start the coal stove to produce heat for the water tank. The hot water was used—and gone—before you could hardly turn around."

With seven people in the family, it was a never-ending chore.

Without electrical power, the thought crossed Isabel's mind she may need to "re-enlist" the glass washboard for laundry. She was relieved when a better option was offered by the head keeper.

This image, taken from the light tower, shows the four keepers cottages. Each home had a shed in back to store coal. The Garcia River is barely visible just above the boundary fence on the right.

Mr. Williams had a small Kohler generator that produced electricity to run his washing machine. He had extended the wiring to the two homes close to him so they could do the same. Williams generously offered Bill and Isabel the same privilege. Bill installed the motor on their machine and Isabel's laundry chores immediately became more manageable. The three assistant keepers all paid their share of the cost of operating the generator.

Compared to the gale-force winds of Point Sur, the light station at Arena was heaven—home to more moderate breezes. Nonetheless, exposed to the weather as it was, lighthouse wind speeds could soar now and then. "Sometimes the wind blew so hard it was difficult to walk back to the house," Shirley remembered. "My father had to help me back once from the barn."

With the advance of spring in 1938—only months before the Nazi Party in Germany unleashed its evil with a pogrom, *Kristallnacht,* that destroyed 267 synagogues and arrested 30,000 Jewish men—Isabel began to plant her garden. Having grown up on a Maryland farm, she brimmed with anticipation of what a well-cared-for vegetable plot could produce. There was plenty of room and good soil to work with—all of which proved exactly to her liking.

The only question, Isabel would later say, was whether her family, or the gophers, would get most of the vegetables. "I've never seen so many gophers in my life as there were at Point Arena."

Town children could make a living, or at least money for extra treats, if they were skilled gopher hunters. Two enterprising children in Point Arena charged ten cents a kill. Several residents saw that as a bargain and hired them to bag as many gophers as they could. Soon, the youngsters had regular money for cherry cokes at Titus Sweet Shop and a bag of popcorn at the Arena Theater.

But out at the light station, Isabel was on her own. "There were times when I could see the tops of carrots moving back-and-forth and hear the crunching sound of the gopher biting them. And then, it would disappear into the ground. They loved the cabbage roots and potatoes, too."

Offended by this, Isabel set traps. "I got some that way," she said with a smile, "but the process took too long." She employed a second line-of-defense for her garden—Bill's .22-caliber rifle.

"Mom got good with Dad's .22," Dixie said. "She'd see a gopher start to work a plant, get the rifle, and wait until the gopher popped his head out of the hole. That was the end of the gopher."

Still, Isabel had success in growing peas, carrots, cabbages, and potatoes. After the vegetables were picked and cleaned, she would spend days canning. "I remember," wrote Joan, "the cellar stairway shelves and the basement shelves lined with jars of all kinds of vegetables. Mom bought fruit to can and make preserves."

In addition, Bessie, the Owens cow, proved to be an excellent investment as a great producer of milk. The cost of dairy products was high. Tillamook Cheese, made on the Oregon Coast, cost thirty-six cents a pound, Troco Butter thirty-five cents per pound, and milk from Stornetta's Dairy sixty-two cents a gallon ($10.68 in today's currency). With Bessie's contributions, Isabel was able to make all the cheese and butter the family could eat, as well as provide milk for the entire station.

The cow was free to wander the light station. Given the flat nature of the property, she was always easy to spot. But one rainy morning as Isabel headed to the barn to milk her, she discovered Bessie was nowhere in

Isabel and girls with Bessie circa 1939. Shirley holds an actual milk bucket. The twins, Joan and Jean, appear to be holding paint buckets for the photo. (Courtesy of Owens Family)

sight. With bluffs in every direction, it was possible the cow had fallen off the edge and into the ocean.

Isabel searched the rim of the station. Just behind the fog-signal building, she saw her. The cow was stranded. She'd slipped eight feet down the bluff's lip before coming to a stop on the ledge. Isabel called to her, but each time Bessie put her hoof on the bank the soft ground gave way.

Isabel hollered for Bill. Several Coast Guardsmen volunteered to help. Bill tied a rope to the bumper of his newly acquired Packard while the two men eased down the muddy slope, looped the rope around the cow, then pushed from Bessie's "aft end." Bill nudged the car forward. When they reached the top, the rope was loosened and removed. Bessie, completely unfazed, twitched her ears and simply walked away.

The incident underscored the ease with which a pet—or an invest-ment—could disappear off a cliff. Bill was able to pull both back from a precipice that morning and Bessie would live to be milked another day.

Everyone had turns at milking her. Bill started but developed hay fever so badly he had to quit. The two older girls also did some milking. "And when our youngest baby was big enough that I could leave her," said Isabel, "I did the milking."

"I should have been a farmer's wife," she added with a smile.

Bill was well-accustomed to operating the first-order lens housed at the top of the tower here. Including its pedestal, it weighed nearly 11,000 pounds, almost six tons.

Manufactured in 1907 by Barbier, Benard, and Turenne of Paris, the lens projected two white flashes every six seconds. The flashes were so brief that an early Lighthouse Service inspector described them as, "practi-cally instantaneous."

Illuminated by a 750-watt bulb, and magnified by the bullseyes, the light could be seen nineteen miles to sea.

The colossal lens took eight hours to clean. "One man inside and one man outside," said Bill. "Once a week."

The station first received commercial electricity from Pacific Gas and Electric Company in the 1930s. Prior to that, the lens burned a wick with coal oil and the rotation was powered by a drop-weight. Now electrified, keepers were relieved of the rewinding task by the installation of a one-eighth horsepower motor that turned the lens. The station was also equipped with a large Kohler generator that took over automatically in the event power failed, which happened often in the winter.

The lens itself was mounted in a "mercury bath," the frame of which contained nearly five and one-half gallons of mercury weighing about 600 pounds. The mercury provided for a near-frictionless rotation. It could be pushed with one finger. The lens made one revolution every eighteen seconds. By the mid-1940s, the light characteristic would change to one flash 0.8 seconds, eclipse 4.2 seconds, flash 0.8 seconds, eclipse 14.2 seconds. At night, any sea captain seeing that combination knew he was off Point Arena.

Electricity also meant steam power was no longer necessary to operate the fog-signal. The compressed-air two-tone diaphone was now powered by electricity from diesel generators. In fog or heavy weather, mariners listened for a three-second blast, silent one-second, a two-second blast, silent fifty-four seconds.

During the 1930s, additional aids to navigation, called radio beacons, were installed at strategic coastal light stations. The beacons transmitted a radio signal from a metal tower to mark a fixed location and provide direction-finding for ships. Both Point Arena and Point Sur had such towers.

"I didn't care for them too much," Bill said. "You sit down on a six-hour watch and hear that thing goin' all the time, 'beep, beep, beep, beep.' But they were effective. We had letters from captains of ships almost all the way to Honolulu that picked up the signal."

For that reason, during World War II, radio signals at Point Arena and other coastal lights were cut down to transmit across a mere ten-mile radius to prevent enemy vessels from picking the signal up at maximum range.

The station's most important task, of course, was lighting the lantern—one-half hour before sunset.

The barn and smaller fenced corral used for the cow are seen with the light tower dominating the station in the background. (Courtesy of Point Arena Light Keepers)

Working near the lens during daylight hours was a colorful but delicate task. The glass prisms were fragile and prone to scratch or chip. Keepers took exceptional care to avoid any contact from their clothing or tools. At the same time, the rays of the sun passing through the lens would cast dozens of brilliant fragments of refracted light—every color of the spectrum. Still, the keeper's enjoyment of the kaleidoscope-like phenomena lasted only a few seconds into the cleaning process.

On watch, each man not only monitored the proper functioning of the beacon but also scanned the ocean for any sign of approaching fog—day or night. If fog was observed within five miles of the coast, the diaphone was activated. In the old days, keepers had to burn two-thirds of a cord of wood to provide the steam needed to operate the foghorn for a ten-hour period. Now, the process required only the flick of a switch.

The enormous size of the Point Arena first-order lens is evident in this photo. The lens is currently displayed in the fog-signal museum at the station. (Author photo)

Chapter Nine

Turmoil

Just south of town, the Arena Cove Lifeboat Station stood at the ready, awaiting pleas for help from ships in trouble. Built in 1902, it had been part of the United States Life-Saving Service. The importance of commerce that shipped in and out of the Point Arena area warranted such a post. While the sentinel at the light station could mark the coast for seafarers, it could do little in the event of a disabled vessel or wreck. The lifeboat station responded to such accidents.

When called upon, crews had a distinguished history of facing hazardous conditions off the local coast and sending out rescue boats. At Arena Cove, two boats were kept ready in the boathouse. The lifeboats would be pushed down the rail "launchways," into the water, and rowed out to sea.

In 1915, the federal government's Life-Saving Service and the Revenue Cutter Service merged to form the Coast Guard. At that time, the Arena Cove station and the light station north of town functioned

The Arena Cove Lifeboat Station was built in 1902. (Courtesy of Owens Family)

independently, but cooperatively. If the light keepers observed a vessel in distress, a quick phone call to alert the officer and crew at the lifeboat station would result in, during Bill's years, the launch of a motorized lifeboat to come to the aid of ship and crew.

"We had two wrecks in one night," Bill said. "Had one go on the beach just about a half-mile north of the light at the mouth of the Garcia River (pronounced 'Gar-sir' with his accent), just on the other side of it. Then, a ship just south of us went on the rocks and was loaded down with Hill's Brothers coffee. One-pound and five-pound cans. Some of the people in town borrowed every boat they could get, and they went out there and gathered up that coffee. They're probably still drinking that coffee yet."

The other ship had cases of wrist watches on it. Townspeople found those in the water, too. "Some of the grammar school kids would come to school with wrist watches all over their arms," Bill remembered. The lifeboat station rescued both crews with no loss of life.

In the 1930s and '40s, the two stations shared a telephone line with the District Office in San Francisco. Different ring patterns identified which station was being called.

Mail duties fell to Owens. He made the daily run to the post office in town, collecting for both stations, then drove to Arena Cove to deliver the lifeboat station's portion of the mail.

The Owens family now lived, for the first time in their lighthouse years, near an actual town. Point Arena had all the basic amenities: two grocery stores, three service stations, an elementary school, and high school. There were churches, three bars, three hotels, a meat market, sweet shop, and a movie theater.

"We had a jail, too," laughed Isabel. "Right behind the volunteer fire station."

Almost everything was on Main Street. Isabel bought groceries at McMillan's and fabrics at Gilmore's Mercantile. On the west side of Main Street, directly across from Gilmore's, stood the Arena Theater. The cinema showed a movie every Wednesday night, a new movie on Saturday, and a repeat showing on Sunday.

Across Main Street from the theater and down a few storefronts stood Titus Sweet Shop. It was the gathering spot for the town's youth—especially high school-aged students. The shop served sodas and ice cream. In a town where everyone knew everyone, it was *the* gathering spot.

On weekend rainy days, when they couldn't go out to play, the twins would ride with Bill on his mail-run to Point Arena. He'd drop the girls at the sweet shop and continue with the mail.

"We'd see at least one of our friends at our favorite soda shop," said Jean. "We'd have a Coke and visit until Dad was ready to return to the lighthouse."

Point Arena residents were dairy farmers, loggers, ranchers, and fishermen. They were hard working, unpretentious, and persistent in their resolve. This suited Bill and Isabel, who were as rock solid as Point Arena itself.

The three oldest children—Shirley, Sarah, and Dixie—entered school in September 1937. It would be an adjustment from the one-room schoolhouse at Point Sur. Point Arena Elementary had three rooms and nearly 100 students. The Owens girls had been accustomed to one room—and only nine or ten students total. At Point Arena, there could be thirty or more children per classroom.

"There were many more children than I'd ever been around," Shirley said. And the Owens girls did not have Miss Gilbert now. But in time, they adapted.

The school, the teachers, and students became more familiar, then more comfortable, and finally, cherished. Point Arena became the first place that felt like home for the Owens family.

Isabel wanted the girls to have new dresses each year for the start of school. Too expensive to buy, she made them. She purchased fabric at Gilmore's, made her own patterns for the dress each girl chose, then cut and sewed the new dresses.

"Mom made all our clothing," recalled one of the twins, Joan. "Dad made us a teeter-totter, a swing, a floor for our play tent, and a little table and chairs."

The town featured Catholic, Methodist, and Presbyterian churches, all well attended. But as the population decreased, the Methodist and Presbyterian

Twins Jean and Joan in the front yard at Point Arena circa 1938. (Courtesy of Owens Family)

churches decided that one would supply a preacher and the other would conduct the Sunday school classes. Isabel started the children in Sunday school as soon as possible.

The Owens girls got along well with the other children at the station.

"We never had any trouble that way," Isabel said. "We had enough children on the light station to have a baseball team. There were something like fifteen or sixteen all together between the four families."

In contrast to the constrained options of Point Sur, the Owens girls had seemingly limitless activities to pursue: board games, hop-scotch, croquet, badminton, or beachcombing. With the long sidewalk in front of the houses, which stretched clear to the lighthouse, roller skating was always a popular choice—with skates that clamped on their shoes.

Beaches near the station offered no end of surprises. The tide was like a genie released from a bottle—displaying an everchanging series of new treasures upon the sand.

What the tide might bring in overnight, no one knew. In one cave, Shirley found the nameplate of the schooner *Crescent City*, wrecked in 1903 a few miles away from the point.

The tide brought glass balls from Japan to the beaches, a prized find. "Nearly every home in town had at least one," said Jean. The orbs had spent ten years floating across the ocean on the North Pacific Current. Rotting ropes or storms had taken them out to sea.

On summer days, Manchester Beach, just across the Garcia River, was the most likely place to find the Owens sisters. In the afternoon, they'd forage along the brackish-scented shoreline for dry driftwood, light twigs, and enjoy a fire in the sand. Occasionally, they did so too close to the water—a surging wave would douse the flames. Undaunted, the lighthouse girls would retreat and start another. This time, a safer distance away.

The girls always brought potatoes with them from the garden. "We'd put them in with the coals, then watch the flames and listen to the surf," said Jean. When the spuds were piping hot, the children scooped them from the coals and enjoyed their feast.

Movies, too, were a popular outing for the family. Every Saturday night, if Bill wasn't scheduled to be on-watch, the whole family would pile in the car and head to the movies. It was a ritual that lasted throughout their time in Point Arena.

The children's town friends lived within walking distance of each other in Point Arena. But five miles out of town, it was harder for the Owens girls to have friends come to the station.

One birthday, Bill and Isabel purchased the twins bicycles, making a get-together with friends easier. The girls were allowed to make a Saturday or Sunday ride to town and visit.

Friends occasionally visited and stayed with the Owens, such as Mr. and Mrs. Danish of San Francisco. Back row, Isabel, Jean, Joan, and Mr. Danish. Front row, Bill, Shirley, Sarah, and Dixie, circa 1938. (Courtesy of Owens Family)

The 18th District Lighthouse Service, under Captain Rhodes, had been known for excellence, efficiency, and frugality. And the organization kept precise track of its property. When Bill was transferred from Point Conception, the head keeper, R.H. George, wrote a letter to the District Office detailing the property returned by his assistant.

Mr. George's letter listed eighty items, including: one book lighthouse instructions, one garden hoe, one 14-inch file, two stove brushes, one stove poker, one brass dustpan, two floor hairbrushes, and two hand grenades. All government property had to be accounted.

"Every piece of furniture had its own number, and it was recorded in the book," said Isabel. "And if anything got worn out and should be thrown away it had to be surveyed first. And you still couldn't do anything [with it] unless you got an answer back from the District that it was

The light tower's circular stairway had 145 steps and several landings to give keepers a place to pause and rest during their climb to the top. (Author photo)

okay to get rid of it. Burn it up or whatever. The ocean got a lot of stuff."

Light station inspections were usually preceded by a three-to-four-day notice. The keepers worked overtime to ensure every aspect of the station was clean and in good functioning order. The families worked equally hard, cleaning floors, kitchens, closets, and bedrooms.

The station's personnel didn't always know who the inspector would be that day. If it was Rhodes who arrived, tensions were taut as a fiddle. But other times, second-in-command O.L. Jenkins would step out of the car.

"Jenkins was different," Bill said. "He'd come out the station, shake your hand and look you in the eye. Ask how things were going. He'd inspect everything and then sit down and have coffee with you."

The year 1939, when Germany invaded Poland to begin World War II, was bursting with life-changing events for the Owens, ranging from one end of the spectrum to the other. On one hand, Bill and Isabel were expecting their sixth child. But on the other, there was trouble and tension on the station—one challenge that effected the working atmosphere on the light, and another that threatened the very existence of the Lighthouse Service.

An environment of relative harmony between keepers was critical for every individual—and every station. Work relations in the Lighthouse Service were often more "pressurized" than other occupations because there was no getting away from one another; keepers and their families were packed together like sailors on a submarine.

The men worked long and sometimes high-stress hours together. When equipment malfunctioned, keepers were required to spot the problem and apply corrective measures as quickly as possible. If a man needed the help of his colleagues, calls were made to each residence, regardless of the time—day or night—and his colleagues came running. Every ship and mariner depended on this cooperation for their very lives.

When duty shifts were completed, keepers were living next door to one another; in many cases within the same duplex or triplex. If relations between keepers were chafed, there was no escaping.

The head keeper, in addition to his own duties, had the task of supervising the work of his assistants. Most of the time, only a corrective word was needed to address an issue. But there were occasions when an assistant cut corners, was argumentative, or, in worse cases, threatening toward the crew.

Trouble at Point Arena began in 1938. Veteran Elmer Williams had been promoted to the position of principal keeper three years earlier and had managed the station efficiently. But for reasons that remain unclear, a keeper on the station had changed the atmosphere to one of discontent and high tension.

The first assistant keeper was a man with local roots. He'd been born in Point Arena to a pioneering family of the Mendocino Coast and had started with the Lighthouse Service in 1929 at Roe Island. Within a year, he'd been transferred to Point Arena.

By 1938, a storm was brewing at the light station, and the first assistant was at its center. He had serious clashes with his superior, Williams. And in lighthouse circles, he did the unthinkable—he left his post when on-watch. Reports of conflict and negligence at the light station began to pile up at the District Office in San Francisco—on the desk of Captain Rhodes. The superintendent investigated the allegations and wrote a letter [through the keeper] to the first assistant confirming these claims on November 11:

> You are hereby charged with neglect of duty, insubordination, insolence to the Keeper, [and] fomenting violent quarrels with other Assistant Keepers at your station. Evidence submitted to the Superintendent indicates that your neglect of duty has extended over a considerable period of time. Specifically, on January 27, 1938, you reported the light out at intervals from 7:30 p.m. to 7:45 p.m. due to Kohler generator troubles, and on June 25, 1938, you reported the light out from 8:00 p.m. to 8:10 p.m., due to the Kohler generator having stopped.
>
> There is no official record of any trouble with the Kohler generating sets at your station, and in case of trouble it would require but a few seconds for the keeper on-watch to throw the switch from the generator to the battery so that there would be no occasion for the

light being extinguished more than a few seconds.

On the occasions mentioned above, it is reported that you were in your quarters at the time instead of standing your watch in the fog signal building as directed, and that on both occasions the Third Assistant Keeper called you by telephone at your quarters and notified you that the light was extinguished. The [Head] Keeper reports that on many occasions you have left your post of duty and gone to your quarters when both the fog-signal and light were in operation, leaving these important aides unattended.

On September 21, 1938, when Mr. H.A. Lang, Junior Engineer, called upon the Keeper for assistance in making measurements in connection with the road work at the station, you were called at 9:20 A.M. after you should have reported for duty, and it was found that you were still in bed. The Keeper further reports that such delinquency on your part was not at all unusual.

Instructions previously given you by both the Superintendent and the Assistant Superintendent to clean your garage, coal shed and yard, have been neglected and incompletely carried out. The Keeper and Assistant Keepers at your station have reported that in addition to improperly carrying out the Keeper's instructions, you have been openly insolent to [the Keeper], and that on numerous occasions you have quarreled with the other Assistant Keepers without cause, and that you have frequently threatened them with bodily harm.

You are directed to submit in writing, through the Keeper, within three days, such reply as you desire to make to the charges.

Signed, H.W. Rhodes, Superintendent

Whether a protocol of corrective measures was offered to the first assistant keeper, there is no record. But he resigned from the Lighthouse Service in February of 1939 and soon left the area.

Chapter Ten

Consolidation

The resignation of the first assistant brought a sense of relief to the station. But bad news followed the good: Shortly afterward, the Owens family lost a longtime and treasured friend. Shep, a companion to the family for fourteen years, died early that spring. Her loss wracked the family, particularly the girls, who'd never lived a day without her—or experienced a death before. She was buried on the light station property.

"She'd been with us for so long and was such a good protector of the children at Conception and Point Sur," said Isabel.

But the climate at the light station soon brightened. Bill and Isabel—now age thirty-eight and age thirty-four, respectively—were expecting another child, due in March. They planned to have the baby at home. And since the cottages had no electricity, Bill was busy in his off-duty hours keeping the house well-lit and warm, closing every door, and gathering blankets wherever he could find them.

The local doctor, A.C. Huntley was affectionately known as "Old

Doc Huntley." His son, also a physician, was called "Young Doc Huntley." On March 18, 1939, "Old Doc" arrived at the house; it was time. Later that day, Isabel gave birth to her seventh baby, another girl, at the Owens cottage. Bill and Isabel named her Diana. She was a healthy baby—a relief to the parents since the nearest hospital was forty-eight miles north in Fort Bragg.

"The older girls were delighted to have a baby in the house again," wrote Isabel. The twins, still several months shy of their sixth birthday, knew this was a monumental occasion.

Isabel holds the couple's sixth daughter, Diana, in the summer of 1939. (Courtesy of Owens Family)

"I remember how Dad kept the coal stove in the kitchen heated," said Joan, "so the baby could be washed and wrapped in blankets there."

While every Owens girl could rightfully lay claim to having been *raised* on a light station, young Diana would have the unique distinction as their only child *born* on a light station.

Home life for Isabel became all the more challenging: a new baby and five other daughters hovering about, offering their help. For Bill, it was business as usual. He stood his watches and performed his daily assigned duties. The demands were increased now that the station was a "man-down" with the resignation of the first assistant.

Near the end of April, Elmer Williams was away on leave. There was no first assistant replacement yet, and the other assistant had left for town and not returned. Bill suddenly found himself on a four-man station—and utterly alone.

For nearly forty-eight straight hours, Bill operated the foghorn and light beacon, and stood watch over both navigational aids. As the second day deepened, he felt himself growing weary, wondering if he had the stamina to keep the pace.

That night, just after he had shut down the foghorn, the question was called: he collapsed from exhaustion. But after regaining consciousness, he managed to maintain the watch to the following morning.

His situation, though, remained desperate. He couldn't do it alone; he needed immediate assistance and asked Isabel if she could stand a watch until help arrived.

"I wish I could," she told him, "but I don't see how. I have a new baby, five girls, and a sick husband to take care of—you."

Owens called Captain Rhodes that morning and asked for another man to be sent out. Rhodes didn't have anyone available, so he gave Bill permission to employ someone locally. Bill hired a man from the ranch next to the lighthouse to help until Williams returned from leave.

A week later, Harmon Day, from Point Sur Light Station, was sent up to temporarily assist. Day soon decided Point Arena was a good station and sent in a request to be transferred there permanently.

Bill would have been in line for the promotion, but Day had more seniority. But as much as the new man liked Point Arena Light, he was soon transferred to the Punta Gorda Lighthouse, just south of Cape Mendocino. Another keeper named Mr. Miller (not the one they'd known at Point Sur) was sent to the station. He, too, had more seniority than Bill. Once again, Bill was passed over for the position. When Miller left Point Arena several years later, Bill was finally promoted to first assistant.

Although relief help had arrived, Bill had still not fully recovered from his two-day non-stop ordeal. He went to see the government physician in Mendocino. The doctor believed Bill's heart to be weak and prescribed Digitalis to regulate his pulse and stimulate the heart muscle. By October, Bill was feeling even worse. He was examined at the Marine Hospital in San Francisco and found to have Digitalis poisoning. He was allergic to the drug that was supposed to help improve his health.

But there was more to come. As the summer of 1939 approached, the turbulent winds that had earlier swept across the Point Arena Light Station became a typhoon. Every light station—and every keeper—in the United States would soon feel the staggering effects.

The United States Lighthouse Service had operated under the Commerce or Treasury Departments for many decades. But the Great Depression had caused the federal government to tighten its belt wherever possible. One cost-saving avenue enacted by Congress was President Franklin Roosevelt's Reorganization Act. It allowed for the consolidation of certain government services, including transferring the United States Lighthouse Service duties to the Coast Guard.

Every man who worked at a lighthouse was shaken by the news; they weren't sure exactly how it would affect them, but it created a fear in each keeper—one that proved justified. The future of lighthouse personnel across the country was now in serious peril. Those in the Lighthouse Service had been hopeful the proposed "folding-in" of the USLHS could somehow be avoided. But on July 7, 1939, it happened.

"A lot of the men were panicky," said Isabel. "They heard rumors that all the lighthouse men would be fired, moved off, and the Coast Guard would put their own enlisted men in. And that they would lose their retirement. It was a rough time. Nobody really knew what to expect."

There were rumors the men would be fired unless they enlisted in the Coast Guard. Many didn't want to. Another rumor suggested a keeper's lighthouse service would no longer count toward retirement.

The uncertainty the men faced lasted until the Secretary of the Treasury, Henry Morganthau, received counsel from the United States Attorney General Frank Murphy. Murphy, later appointed by Roosevelt to the Supreme Court, received a letter from Morganthau on June 22, 1939. The secretary had written Murphy for his legal opinion related to the status of the Lighthouse Service personnel in "the transfer and consolidation of the Lighthouse Service with the Coast Guard…effective July 1, 1939."

> Your opinion is requested (1) whether personnel of the Lighthouse Service entitled to retirement benefits at the present time will be entitled to such benefits after July 1, 1939, and (2) whether the above cited retirement statutes will be applicable to personnel of the Lighthouse Service, now eligible (except as to age and length of service),

who will perform in the Coast Guard the same or similar duties which
they are now performing in the Lighthouse Service.

In his response four days later, Murphy referred to a recommendation by the Committee on Interstate and Foreign Commerce that noted
the enactment of the amendment of May 22, 1926, "and its intent to
provide for the retirement of lighthouse personnel."

Murphy's review of the amendment led him to conclude, "It appears
that, because of the hazardous nature of the service, it was the purpose of
the Congress to provide for certain employees in [the Lighthouse] Service retirement privileges similar to those which had been provided for
the Coast Guard.

> Without further legislation, however, Lighthouse Service employ-
> ees of the classes eligible for retirement under the Lighthouse Retire-
> ment Act will not ... be eligible for retirement under the special
> statutes relating to the retirement of Coast Guard personnel. There-
> fore, unless the Lighthouse Retirement Act remains applicable, such
> employees will be denied privileges which the Congress clearly
> intended they should have.
>   It is my opinion, therefore, that the answer to both questions pre-
> sented should be in the affirmative."

A copy of this important exchange was sent to H.D. King, the Commissioner of Lighthouses. King then forwarded it to all Superintendents
of Lighthouses across America, including Harry Rhodes. On June 29,
1939, Rhodes sent a copy of the opinion to all those under his supervision.

With the backing of the Attorney General, it appeared the lighthouse men would be able to continue their employment under the Coast
Guard while remaining eligible for their retirement benefits. However,
any job vacancies created by promotion, retirement, or death would be
now filled by Coast Guard personnel.

Some men believed by enlisting they'd have better job security and
higher pay in the Coast Guard. Others wanted to remain civil servants.
But one thing was undeniable: The Bureau of Lighthouses was going
out of existence, its duties assimilated into the operations of the United
States Coast Guard.

Rhodes wanted none of it—not one day of it. After forty-one years of government service—twenty-seven with the Lighthouse Service—he retired July 7, the day the Coast Guard took over.

Lighthouse personnel were given the option of entering the Coast Guard through a military position or remaining Civil Service employees. The split was half-and-half. Bill wouldn't enlist—at least not now. What he didn't know was that the U.S. was soon going to war, and that would change everything. Not that more minor changes wouldn't occur as soon as the shift took place.

One of the most difficult for Bill to swallow was having to take direction from the Coast Guard on how the lights should be run and operated. It was the keepers who were seasoned campaigners in the field of light keeping—not the Coast Guard. The entire process had left the men from the Lighthouse Service feeling disrespected, ignored, and exploited.

"Those Coast Guard screwballs didn't know a thing about operating a light station," Bill said. "And here, they would come in and tell us how to do our job. Roosevelt thought the same personnel that was running the Coast Guard could also run the lighthouses, but he was wrong."

Now, the lifeboat and light stations were under the same bureaucratic umbrella and, at times, at odds with one another. Neither wanted to be under the authority of the other. And when the USLHS was swallowed by the Coast Guard, the lighthouse men became vulnerable.

"The Coast Guard guys over at the lifeboat station were all arguing with each other about who was going to come over and get such-and-such quarters," Bill recalled.

"There were four quarters there at Point Arena," said Isabel. "And all of them were four-bedroom houses. Over at the lifeboat station, they had a house for the commanding officer to live in, and barracks for the single fellows. But the married men had to rent any kind of shack they could find down close to the station. And that's about what they were—shacks. The men there were deciding among themselves who was going to have which house. But it didn't work out."

In defense of his keepers, Elmer Williams, the head keeper at the light station until 1940, crossed swords with the commander of the lifeboat station. Upon Williams' transfer, the new head keeper, Oliver Berg,

Bill, in Coast Guard uniform, is second from left. The station crew are having some fun with soda pop delivered by the USO circa 1943. (Courtesy of Point Arena Light Keepers)

took up the departmental in-fighting, always protecting the men of the light station.

Berg and his wife had been serving at Farallon Island, where he had been head keeper. The Bergs thought the transfer to the mainland might prove a pleasant change from the remoteness of the island twenty-seven miles off the coast of San Francisco. But the move didn't bring the satisfaction they had anticipated.

"We knew the Bergs well," said Isabel. "I think they missed the islands. Mrs. Berg always talked about her life there."

Hetty Berg had indeed been fond of their unique life on Farallon. It was an old station, first lit in 1855. The lighthouse was built atop the highest peak on the island. A long trail of switchbacks led up to the tower.

"I learned to love the islands," Mrs. Berg later wrote. "We were a congenial bunch, and all the islanders would go abalone hunting together. For evening amusement, we would gather at the home of one of the keepers or at the wireless station and play cards—or wind up the phonograph and dance."

The lighthouse tender *Lupine* called biweekly at Farallon Island during the Berg's years there, delivering food, mail, coal, fuel, and other supplies. Keepers' wives wrote in for groceries every two weeks. When the meat supply ran low there was always good fish from the sea.

"Boat Day was like a holiday for us. We were up early and down to the dock to be on time when the tender arrived."

During their years at Point Arena, the Bergs would be a steadying influence after the tumultuous times of 1938 and '39. Between the forced resignation of the first assistant, consolidation of the Lighthouse Service, and the drum beat of war in Europe, Point Arena's personnel needed Berg's leadership—and they got it.

Chapter Eleven

Blackouts and Beach Patrols

Within a year of Bill's arrival at Point Arena the world had begun to unravel. In Europe, the chances of war increased with every demand and threat from Adolph Hitler. In March 1938, the German Fuhrer annexed Austria in what would be known as the "Anschluss," or "joining," of the country to the German Reich. This was soon followed by Hitler pressuring for the cession of Czechoslovakia's Sudetenland, declaring it "the last territorial demand I have to make in Europe."

British Prime Minister Neville Chamberland met with Hitler in Berchtesgaden, Germany, on September 15 and, along with leaders from France, Italy, and Germany, agreed to the annexation of the Sudeten to the Reich. The Munich Agreement was signed on September 30, 1938.

Later that day, the British leader returned to the Heston Airport in London. Mobbed by large crowds, Chamberlain held aloft a copy of the agreement, "symbolic," he said, "of the desire of our two countries never to go to war with one another again." As the paper fluttered in the wind, he added, "Here is the paper which bears his name upon it as well as mine."

The same evening in Berlin, Hitler told his foreign minister, Joachim von Ribbentrop, not to be concerned with the agreement. "That piece of paper is of no further significance whatever," he said.

Chamberland's claim of "peace in our time" was a mirage; it disappeared as the Nazis invaded Poland on September 1, 1939. Two days later, Great Britain and France declared a state of war now existed with Germany.

Meanwhile in the Far East, Japan had begun a series of aggressions to establish a Pacific Empire. Japanese troops had invaded areas of China and Southeast Asia, which the country's forces now occupied.

But Japan had much larger aspirations. On December 7, 1941, the Japanese launched a devastating surprise attack on the U.S. Pacific Fleet at Pearl Harbor, leaving 2,334 military personnel dead—and the fleet in flames. That same day, Japan attacked the Philippine Islands, the Dutch East Indies (today's Indonesia), Thailand, Malaysia, Hong Kong, and the Shanghai International Settlement in China.

In the days following the December 7 assault on Pearl Harbor, nine Japanese submarines assigned to sail east from Hawaiian waters had arrived at strategic positions along the West Coast of North America. Immediately, the hunting of U.S. merchant ships began.

On December 18, the freighter *Samoa* was attacked off Cape Mendocino by the Japanese sub *I-17*. The *Samoa* miraculously escaped with little damage and safely reached the port of San Diego. Two days later, the SS *Agwiworld* was sighted by another submarine, the *I-23*, twenty miles off Cypress Point, near Monterey. The ship eluded the shelling from the submarine's deck gun with the aid of heavily pitching seas and use of a thick smoke screen.

On December 20, the tanker SS *Emidio* was enroute from Seattle to San Francisco when she was attacked by the Japanese submarine *I-17* off Cape Mendocino, 200 miles north of San Francisco.

The sub shelled the tanker with a deck gun, then drove a torpedo into the stern of the ship and submerged. Thirty-one members of the crew were rescued but six others died in the attack. The badly crippled

Emidio remained afloat for several days, drifting north until she finally washed upon rocks at Crescent City, near the Oregon-California border.

Several days before the *Emidio* was attacked, Bill Owens had been on-watch at the fog-signal building when he spotted a submarine off Point Arena. "It was real early in the morning. I saw it come up out of the water right in front of the light. I didn't report it as a Japanese submarine because I didn't know what it was. All I knew was it was a submarine. So, I grabbed the phone and called Navy headquarters and reported it. We had to report everything to the Navy then."

"They told me, 'There are no subs up north. Go back to bed and get some more sleep.'"

"Well, a day or two later a submarine put a torpedo through the *Emidio*—killed several people north of Fort Bragg. A bunch of Navy officers came up the next day and swore me to secrecy. I wasn't to tell anybody that I had reported it. I said, 'How long do I have to keep quiet?' And they said, 'Till the war is over.' So, I didn't tell anybody till the war was over. Then I told everybody."

Japanese submarine attacks didn't end with the *Emidio*. On the morning of December 23, the *I-21* spotted the Union Oil tanker SS *Montebello* heading north to deliver over three million gallons of oil to Vancouver, British Columbia—a destination the ship would never reach. At 5:45 A.M., a torpedo carrying an 893-pound warhead from the Japanese sub exploded on the Montebello's starboard side. The vessel sank an hour later, though all aboard were saved.

The sinkings continued into 1942. Attacks included the shelling of the oil fields, piers, and derricks at Ellwood, California, near Santa Barbara. The *I-17* surfaced in the dark at 7 P.M. on February 23, and lobbed shells at the oil facility for twenty minutes. Little damage was inflicted, but the captain, Kozo Nishino, had achieved his primary goal of spreading fear among the residents of coastal California.

The West Coast was under the impending threat of foreign forces attacking harbors and coastal shipping. Lighthouse personnel were immediately put on alert to keep a watchful eye for any enemy warships. Shortly after the attack on the *Emidio*, a communique entitled "Submarine Sighting Check List" was distributed to each lighthouse.

It contained fourteen points of observation. Among them were time and date, course and speed of the sub, size and superstructure, and side numerals. Additional questions asked the observer if the vessel was surfacing or diving. Was there a bow wake? Was the sub signaled? What action did it take?

Buildings that could be seen from the sea were required to "black-out" their lights at night. Streetlights, advertising and commercial lights, and residential and industrial windows were included in the nightly "dimout," as it was sometimes referred to. Lights on the Golden Gate Bridge were masked or shielded on the seaward side.

But as did other coastal sentinels, the Point Arena Lighthouse lens kept shining, its beacon visible far out to sea. All other buildings at the light station were to have their windows covered and their lights turned out when a door was opening—a requirement that rankled Bill.

"The light was never blacked out," he said. "Here's this big light going full-blast—a 390,000-candlepower light you can see nineteen-miles away—and we couldn't show a light in our house." Then he added, shaking his head, "Screwballs."

Isabel found the circumstances as ironic as her husband. "We had to have curtains pulled on the windows. You couldn't open the door until the light was turned off. You had to drive your car with the parking lights only. You could barely see the road."

At the time, Diana was only three years old. "I didn't realize the seriousness of it. To me, it was just exciting seeing everyone rushing around covering the windows."

There were times when the lighthouse was the only light shining over seventy-five-miles of coastline. Nighttime activities were curtailed. High school athletic games were played during the day. Sunday night movie showings were changed to matinees.

Planes were constantly flying past the light station—day and night. "When we heard the engines," said Shirley, "we'd wonder if the planes were ours or theirs. There were times we were frightened, especially when we were notified to be ready to leave at a moment's notice. I sometimes wondered what would happen to us if an enemy ship tried to shell the light and missed."

The Point Arena light tower beaming in the night. The radio beacon tower can barely be seen to the left.

In a sense, the lighthouse was the most *unsafe* place along the coastline—a place that essentially advertised to the Japanese: *We're here. You can't see anything else at night but us!*

———

With the beginning of the war, Americans worried over the security of their coastline—with good reason. By striking Hawaii, the Japanese had already demonstrated the long arm of the empire's military capability. They quickly proved their reach extended even further—all the way to America's West Coast as the Japanese attacked shipping within view of California's shore.

Now, authorities worried about small enemy sabotage groups landing on American's seaboards. Fears that Nazi or Japanese submarines could surface and land soldiers or agents prompted the need for coastal beach patrols.

The risk was real. On America's East Coast, the Germans launched "Operation Pastorius" in June 1942. Eight men, trained in sabotage, had been ferried by U-boats to the shores of New York and Florida. Their mission was to disrupt war industries and create a wave of terror by planting explosives in public buildings. Plans included destroying a hydroelectric plant at Niagara Falls, the Alcoa Aluminum plants in Tennessee and New York, locks on the Ohio River, and the Hell Gate Bridge over the East River.

The mission failed, and all eight agents were arrested. George Dasch, a German national who had spent extensive time in the United States, was the commander of the teams. He betrayed his men by turning himself in to the FBI in Washington D.C.

The beach patrols established along both shores were not intended as military protection of the Pacific and Atlantic coastlines. Rather, they were outposts, patrols whose functions were rescue and policing of restricted areas.

Manned by Coast Guardsmen and volunteers, nearly 3,700 miles of coastline was "watched" between 1942 and 1945. The chain of Coast Guard lifeboat stations, lighthouses, and lookouts formed the core of a coastal communication system along each seaboard. Patrols often consisted of one man with a rifle, a trained dog or horse, and a radio or flare pistol for communication.

The population on the Point Arena light station changed dramatically with the onset of the war. What had been a quiet post with four keepers and their families became a station teeming with personnel. Eventually, there were sixty-four men on the station at one time.

"When they sent in the last twenty-six [men], Mr. Berg had me talk to the senior Petty Officer. I told him, 'You're runnin' your own crew here. We're not gonna fool with their liberties and so forth. All we'll do, we'll feed you here.'"

The Navy provided a cook and all the food necessary.

At Point Arena, beach patrols consisted of Coast Guardsmen, often in pairs, walking two-mile sections of beach, traversing back-and-forth over six-hour shifts. Some men rode horses. At isolated posts along the Pacific Coast, men cut new trails to beaches and coves and did their own cooking. Point Arena, by comparison, was an easy assignment.

The so-called "beach pounders" who scattered north and south of the light station were composed of modestly equipped guardsmen. They had M-1 rifles, .45-caliber handguns, and plenty of ammunition.

The ever-present sound of the ocean breakers—like soft static on a radio—and the gentle grind of boots across the sand created the only sounds on patrol—except on windy days, or days when rain whipped at horizontal angles, which were frequent during winter. Then, the sound of a man's own shivering could be heard, as the chill of January temperatures seeped to his bones.

At some locations, the men conducted patrols only at night. But in areas where potential for landings or sabotage activities was greater—such as the major harbors at San Diego, Los Angeles, San Francisco, or Seattle—around-the-clock vigilance was required.

Adding to the coastal surveillance were Army and Navy planes which flew countless missions along the West Coast, scanning the waters for any sign of enemy ships or submarines. Suspicious wakes were given second and third looks. Though the Navy had disbanded the large dirigible program after the Macon crash, small blimps were employed to crisscross the shoreline or escort military and merchant vessels. The LTA's were a common sight off the shores of Point Arena.

"Some blimps passed very close to the station," recalled Isabel.

At the beginning of the war, the U.S. Navy had only ten blimps capable of coastal anti-submarine patrols. But soon, more than 200 would join the fleet. Major Naval Air Station bases for LTA's were located at Santa Ana in southern California, Sunnyvale, California (Moffett Field), and Tillamook, Oregon. Auxiliary stations were located at Arcata and Eureka in northern California.

The crafts were hardly intended for heavy combat. The common blimp was armed with a single .50-caliber machine gun and four depth-bombs hanging from racks beneath their control cars. Crews were ordered to monitor the positions of friendly ship traffic and report any sightings of enemy submarines that could then be attacked by patrolling warships or fighter planes from Naval Air Stations.

This 1943 photo, taken from the front steps of the family's cottage at Point Arena, shows how the Owens girls were growing up. (Courtesy of Owens family)

Bill had enlisted in the Coast Guard in October 1942. Because it was war time, he felt a duty to do so—albeit with the intention of returning to civil service once the war was over. The station was now under military control, and he would have been required to enlist anyway to continue his work at the lighthouse. Glad to be able to remain at the station in his role, Bill was nonetheless still frustrated at times by the Coast Guard handling, or mishandling, of the lights and personnel.

The month after Bill had been made Bosun Mate First Class in 1943, he was ordered to San Francisco for training on being a lighthouse keeper. "I'd been a lighthouse keeper for twelve years by then!" he said with a wry smile.

Coast Guard "harassment" of the Lighthouse Service men, or at least how it felt to them, sometimes surfaced in inspection notifications. Often, only one day of warning was received—or less. Phone calls announcing a surprise inspection sometimes occurred on the "morning of."

"It always seemed to happen on a school day," wrote Joan. "We'd be getting ready for school and Mom would be in the middle of making breakfast and preparing our lunches. Some of us would be getting dressed while others were waiting their turn in the bathroom."

The phone would ring. "Officers will be there for inspection in an hour."

"Then," said Dixie, "we'd clean the kitchen, bedrooms, living room—everything. As fast as we could."

At times, the lighthouse men believed the Coast Guard had adopted a strategy that said, in essence, "If we make life uncomfortable enough for these lighthouse guys, maybe they'll just quit." Small issues, not worthy of mentioning, would be pointed out—perhaps with the intent to simply "tweak" the former USLHS keepers. It was never appreciated at the receiving end.

On one occasion, Bill met two officers who arrived at Point Arena for such an inspection. As they passed the station truck, the officers noticed there were no valve stem caps on the tires. Insignificant as it was, they decided to press the issue with Bill.

"You know it's Coast Guard regulations the station's truck should have caps on the valve stems."

"They were lost," said Bill.

The officers looked again at the tires before walking to the fog-signal building to examine the equipment inside. The minute they entered and were out of earshot, Owens summoned one of his men.

"Take the valve caps off their tires, throw them away—and then get lost."

Bill quickly caught up with the officers and accompanied them during the examination of the fog-signal and tower. As they exited the base of the lighthouse, Owens paused, looked at the wheels of the officer's vehicle, and casually mentioned, "I notice you don't have stem caps either."

What the officers thought of this, there was no telling. But they said nothing more about stem caps.

As Coast Guard personnel flooded the light station in 1942, the young men needed housing. The commander crammed them in the empty keepers dwelling next to the Owens home and the Quonset huts at the nearby LORAN (short for "long range navigation") station.

That decision was received differently within the Owens house—depending on whether one's perspective was that of a parent, or a teenage daughter.

Isabel was less than pleased. "The service men were away from home for the first time in their lives—and didn't have their fathers watching over them. And there they were—living right next to me with five teenagers."

Bill knew this would mean exercising extra vigilance in managing both the service men and his and Isabel's daughters. In contrast, the young females in the Owens household were delighted, as were most of their friends.

Shirley would later write, "The house next door to us was turned into a single men's barracks for Coast Guard men. That was exciting. All those young men resulted in some of my classmates at high school wanting to visit us."

The twins, then nine-years-old, were equally enthusiastic. "Jean and my bedroom faced the barracks and we used to spend hours in the dark watching the men play pool and sitting in their kitchen talking."

Bill kept a close eye on the girls. And, given his knack for bluntness, it's a good bet the keeper had warned the men to stay clear of his daughters.

The local boys of Point Arena didn't like the young servicemen. "The Coast Guard men had money to date all the girls," Isabel said. "The parents didn't trust the Coast Guard fellows either." Whether that parental mistrust was well-founded or not, Isabel would only laugh.

The teenagers had always enjoyed having Diana, three-years-old when the war began, follow wherever they went. But now, there were young men to chat with on the lighthouse grounds—and Diana was suddenly persona non grata.

"I was the tag-along who couldn't understand why I wasn't welcome anymore when my sisters and some of the guys at the station would be talking."

Isabel with her daughters out to pick wild strawberries at the light station in 1942. From left are Jean, Joan, Dixie, Sarah, Shirley, Isabel, and, in front, Diana. (Courtesy of Owens family)

With war raging across the globe, and particularly with the Japanese presence off the coast, some Point Arena families were reluctant to allow their children to visit the station. "Most of the parents thought it would be more dangerous for their children to be at the light station if the Japanese happened to shell us," said Dixie.

The parental worry was reasonable given the enemy action along the coast. A Japanese submarine, the *I-26*, had shelled the lighthouse at Estevan Point, Vancouver Island, on June 20, 1942. The following night, Fort Stevens on the northern Oregon Coast was attacked by the *I-25's* five-inch deck gun.

The United States government also feared potential Japanese bombings of West Coast communities. In September 1942, a sub surfaced off the southern coast of Oregon. Pilot Nobuo Fujita catapulted off the deck of the *I-25* in a Glen Floatplane. Fujita's mission was to drop an incendiary bomb on Wheeler Ridge, east of Brookings, in hopes of setting the forest aflame. At the end of September, he dropped another bomb just east of the coastal town of Port Orford. Both bombs exploded, but the fires were quickly extinguished by personnel at forest service lookouts.

Another bombing resulted in the first—and only—civilians to die on the U.S. mainland during World War II. Japanese scientists had calculated that large high-altitude balloons carrying explosives could reach the continental United States—riding the jet stream—in two to three days. The balloons were able to adjust for altitude changes until reaching the mainland. Upon landing, an incendiary bomb would explode to create a forest fire, the Japanese hoped. Japan released a flurry of balloon bombs—eventually over 9,000. Most balloons "died" at sea, while others were shot down by fighter planes as they were detected. But some got through. The government later estimated 1,000 reached the United States, generally in the Pacific Northwest.

One day in the last year of the war, 1945, Reverend Archie Mitchell and his pregnant wife, Elsie, drove to Gearhart Mountain, fifty miles northeast of the southern Oregon town of Klamath Falls. With them were five children from their Sunday school class. After dropping off his wife and the children, Mitchell moved the car to a parking area. As he returned, he witnessed a nightmare. His wife and the children had stumbled across a large, deflated balloon lying on the ground. One child kicked the object, and the bomb exploded. Four children died instantly in the blast while a fifth, along with Mrs. Mitchell, died minutes later. It was later concluded the balloon had drifted to the ground several weeks before and lain undisturbed until the group of youngsters discovered it.

The possibility of civilian casualties from enemy bombing led the government to train workers in fingerprinting. Bill Owens was among them. He had a framed certificate upon his wall from the Institute of Applied Science indicating he had successfully completed training. Bill fingerprinted every child in Point Arena for civil files. The motive behind it was chilling: so children's bodies could be identified if the schools were bombed.

Concerns over bombings and shellings lasted only until the war's end. Then, parents felt safe in allowing their children to visit the light station. Not long after the Japanese surrender on September 2, 1945, the *Mendocino Beacon* ran a short story reporting that "Mrs. William Owens gave a pajama party for the girls of the 8th grade at her home at Point Arena lighthouse. A wonderful time was had by all."

Every girl in Jean and Joan's class attended, a symbolic indication that whatever innocence the war had robbed from those along the California coast was now back.

———

During the summer of 1945, Oliver Berg retired. By then, Bill had been his first assistant for three years. With Oliver's retirement, the baton was passed. Bill's devotion to duty through the Depression and a World War was finally rewarded. In August, he was promoted to officer-in-charge at Point Arena.

In December, Bill left the Coast Guard and returned to civilian status. The civilian keepers would still be in line for promotions as openings became available. But each year, through attrition, the dynamic changed as the ratio of former lighthouse men to the Coast Guard dwindled. Still, Washington, D.C., would have the final say concerning any action involving the civilian lighthouse personnel—a directive Bill would soon find himself depending on.

As the joyous post-war celebrations faded, Point Arena's light station returned to its pre-war ambiance. Dozens of military personnel left the station, and the lighthouse reservation returned to its normal compliment of staff. Lighthouse duties remained numerous—from cleaning to painting, from maintenance to repair, the men were kept busy. But on a keeper's off-hours, he could do as he pleased. Bill's pleasure was to fish for salmon, usually on the Garcia River.

One day at the light station, he was walking among the rocks at the water's edge when something odd caught his attention. He had been looking for abalone. What he found in the water was a piece of history. Peering through the surface, he spotted a large white stone of some sort, a few feet below. Minding his balance as he waded knee-deep into the icy water, he realized the object was man-made. Bill's own curiosity urged him on. He tied one end of a rope to the object and the other to the bumper of his car. Slowly, he nudged forward to pull his find out of the water and atop the bluff.

It was a concrete arch with writing engraved upon it:

Point Arena Lighthouse
Erected 1870
Lt. Col. R.S. Williamson
L.H. Engr.

Owen's discovery turned out to be the lintel, or doorway span, from the original 1870 lighthouse. It had been shoved into the ocean in 1906—along with the other earthquake rubble. What were the chances that a lighthouse keeper would find a symbol of the very place he worked—under water, no less? Williamson's name was familiar to Bill since his days at Point Conception. To Owens, the lintel was a treasure worthy of being preserved. He made a concrete base and cemented the arch in place a few feet east of the current light tower—where it remains today.

Not long after Bill took command of the station, the Coast Guard requested all lighthouse logbooks be collected and sent to the District Office. Little value seemed to be placed on them and the Coast Guard, at the time, was not known for having an interest in preserving lighthouse history. Some logbooks made their way to Washington, D.C. archives.

The lintel of the original lighthouse built in 1870. It had been under water since the 1906 earthquake. (Author photo)

Many were burned or simply disappeared.

Bill collected and stored the logs in his office. The old records generally listed the daily work completed at the station—or if there had been anything unusual in the operation of the light or fog-signal.

But from time to time, additional information seeped into the record. "I looked through some of them before they were shipped in," remembered Isabel. "They were interesting. A couple got married up in the light tower once. Back in the 1890s there had been an epidemic at Point Arena, and the light station sent someone every day to help take care of the sick. Another recorded a bear being sighted at the station."

On at least one occasion, Bill found the logs to be a useful reference source. He'd received a letter from a man requesting help in acquiring his birth certificate. The letter-writer said he'd been born on the Point Arena Light Station. Bill began to dig through the logs, found when he was born, and wrote back confirming the date of his birth at the station. Bill soon received a thank-you note; the man finally had his birth certificate.

———

The Owens girls were changing—and maturing. Shirley was now seventeen years old; Sarah and Dixie sixteen and fifteen, respectively. All three were high school students and growing into young women faster than their parents could believe.

The younger girls were still in their playful stages. The twins were twelve years old, and Diana had now turned six. Joan took piano lessons and Diana soon followed in her steps. For them, skating and hop-scotch were still favored pastimes.

For everyone, school was a priority. Now, with Diana's entry in kindergarten the year before, all six girls were attending school at the same time, causing long lines at home waiting for the bathroom as the kids readied to leave each morning.

Bill had tackled the early years of transporting the children to and from school. But given his duties at the light station at Point Arena, necessity required another driver—and Isabel was the obvious candidate. Bill taught her on the light station. Whether he was a harsh teacher

Bill Owens on the gallery outside the lens room at Point Arena. (Courtesy of Owens family)

or she a lag-behind student was later a topic of debate between the two. But over the years, it would be Isabel who taught every Owens daughter how to drive.

"I didn't want anyone to go through what I did," Isabel said, smiling.

There was plenty of local driving to be done. Trips back-and-forth to town were daily rituals. Bill had the Coast Guard truck for the mail run. Isabel drove the Packard for the rest.

Children in town could catch the school bus to campus. But those living at the lighthouse, or on ranches and dairies on the outskirts of Point Arena, were on their own.

She ferried children from the station to the school every day, then picked up another six or seven children at Brush Opening, about three miles east of town. Later, she was asked to pick up children at the Rancheria—the Pomo Indian Reservation. If you lived far away, the county paid parents enough to cover the gas to bring their children in for school.

The Owens car had three rows of seats and each seat held three children. All were filled.

"Mom picked up kids twice a day," Jean testified. "How in the world she managed to have any time for herself is beyond my imagination."

Chapter Twelve

Great Lamentation

The ocean off Point Arena was both generous and unmerciful. There were times of great abundance for fishermen and gentle days for beachcombers. And there were horrific hours when a ship and her crew were merely bones to be chewed and spit ashore.

Planes were also at risk over the coastal waters. On August 7, 1946, Bill was on-watch when a commercial fisherman radioed that his engine had broken down and needed help. The Coast Guard was out all night looking for him.

The following day, a twin-engine Catalina Flying Boat was searching for the missing vessel. Shortly after 2:30 P.M., Bill, while outside, watched the plane plying up and down the coast, skimming just above the waves—and witnessed a catastrophe.

The plane was flying low, a half-mile offshore. An ocean swell suddenly rose and caught one of the pontoons of the Catalina. The wing plunged sharply into the water. The plane cartwheeled and exploded in a plume of water and flames. Six Coast Guard men died in an instant.

"I called the Coast Guard and they sent out lifeboats," Bill said. "They picked up one man; he'd been blown right through the cabin. Still had his bucket seat on. The plane sank within five minutes."

During the next few hours, two additional bodies were recovered before fog and darkness temporarily prevented further searching.

Several Owens children witnessed the crash, a memory they would never forget. "My sister, Jean, and I had been to the beach," Diana recalled. "We were coming back across the field when we heard an airplane. We saw it come down and crash near the mouth of the Garcia River. Later, the parents of one of the boys came to the station to talk to Dad. They wanted to know what had happened and where it occurred. I was sent out to play as it was a difficult and very sad discussion."

Bill remembered the visit from the parents. "This one boy's folks were from the Midwest. They'd been walking up and down the beach all day. I told 'em, 'You just as well go home.'

"A few days later, a woman came rushing over to our house. 'A body just washed in on the beach over there! A drowned man!' I went over and it was the boy from the Midwest. His parents had just left the day before."

The fishing vessel the Coast Guard men had been searching for seemed to have disappeared. But several days later, the craft was discovered—safely tied to a dock in San Francisco Bay.

———

Each light keeper was given vacation time. Respite from the constant round-the-clock watches and station work was much needed and anticipated.

Nearly each summer, Bill and Isabel would pack up the girls, food, tent, and camping equipment. Their camping experiences in Big Sur had been rejuvenating and they continued the practice soon after arriving at Point Arena. Bill had discovered a spot just up the Garcia River that bordered the lighthouse reservation. He would take thirty days of vacation every year, during which the district office would send a man up to take his place.

There were times Owens didn't approve of the quality of work performed in his absence, though he fondly remembered a young man who proved to be an exceptional replacement. "I finally got a man, a real nice fellow—married. And he wanted to go to college once he was finished with the Coast Guard. But, boy, if I went up to there today, I'd know he had the station running good all the time I was away. Later, he'd ask me to write letters of recommendation for him. He became a college professor."

The family's favorite spot was called "Holiday's." Among the towering redwoods were several cabins and camping spaces. The family always looked forward to a two-week break from the fog. The girls hiked and played in the water hole. Everyone enjoyed eating meals cooked outdoors and gathering around a campfire in the evening.

Looking back as adults, the Owens daughters wondered if camping may not have been as delightful for Isabel as it had been for them. "Mom didn't get away from her 'wifely chores'," Joan remembered. "There was still cooking, cleaning, washing dishes, and bandaging our scrapes."

Camping at Holiday's near the Garcia River in the summer of 1942. Back left is Dixie, Shirley, and Sarah. Front row is Joan, Isabel, Diana, Bill, and Jean. (Courtesy of Owens Family)

But camping was every bit to Isabel's satisfaction. She was an outdoor person and while the years may have expunged any unpleasant memories of the associated chores, she enjoyed the family camp—and said she always came back feeling rested and refreshed.

One summer at Holiday's, the family had established their campsite—dominated by a picnic table, wooden shelves, and an enormous green canvas tent—when a young dog came wandering by. Apparently lost, the dog decided he would not leave the Owens camp and slept outside their tent doorway every evening. Each day that passed, the animal ate with the family and followed the girls as they played.

"That little black dog adopted us," said Isabel.

The children reveled in the fun of having a dog that seemed to enjoy them as much as they enjoyed the dog.

No one came looking for him so when it was time to return to the light station, the family packed up the dog along with their belongings. They named him "Pal" and he quickly became a part of the clan.

A month later, Shirley and Sarah were playing in front of the house. A man arrived in a car and stepped out. They'd never seen him before.

"Is your dad around?" he asked.

"I'll get him," said Shirley. "He's down at the fog-signal."

She quickly returned with her father at her side.

The man shook Bill's hand.

"I've been told you might have found a little black dog back on the Garcia. I lost one like that last month."

Just then, the rest of the Owens girls came running around the corner of the fence—with Pal tagging along side.

"That's him, alright. I came to take him home."

The girls were wide-eyed with dread.

It had been a month, and the children had fallen in love with Pal. Eyes welled up with tears.

"He's a good dog," Bill told the man. "And the kids love him. Would you take five dollars to leave him with us?"

The man put his fingers to his chin, as if reluctant. Then he looked at the children.

"Well, sure," he said. "Dog looks like he's got a good home."

The tears were wiped dry from the girls' cheeks, which quickly turned to smiles.

"Yeah!" they shouted, bouncing up and down.

Bill rarely had the chance to be the hero in a family crisis. But the children never forgot the day he arranged for Pal to stay. For years, the dog was a companion and playmate for the children.

"Wherever we went at the lighthouse, he went, too," remembered Jean. "He'd often run ahead, but never too far. And then he'd run back to us."

Pal soon displayed a rare skill. He spotted a mouse in the kitchen one day. The mouse scampered into an open cupboard. Pal dove in right behind him. Pots and pans flew in all directions. But within seconds, the dog backed out of the cabinet with the mouse in his mouth.

From that day on, whenever a mouse was seen in the home, Isabel called for Pal.

And he made quick work of every rodent he saw.

The relationship between Lighthouse Service men and the Coast Guard continued to be strained. The USLHS men believed the Coast Guard officers had little respect for their knowledge and skill. Further, they believed the officers saw them as "easily replaceable." The lighthouse men were under their authority and could only hope they'd be treated fairly. At times, they were not.

In 1945, the Lifeboat Station, the Loran Station, Point Cabrillo Light Station, and Point Arena Light Station were all placed within the same Coast Guard unit. The officer-in-charge of the lifeboat station had overall authority. He decided Bill Owens had been at Point Arena long enough and ordered him to report to Pigeon Point Light Station.

Bill did *not* want to go.

Owens tried repeatedly to reach the Commander of the District, but he was away on leave. Finally, the lifeboat officer told Bill that if he wasn't on his way to Pigeon Point the next morning, he would "send some men over to put him on the bus."

Point Arena was home to Bill and his family; in a sense, it was the only place that had really felt like home. He wanted to stay for Isabel and the children. He wanted to stay for himself.

Just how serious the Coast Guard was about the move was evidenced by the *Mendocino Beacon's* reporting that "Bill Owens, officer-in-charge after eight years at the Point Arena Lighthouse, has been transferred. He reports to Pigeon Point next week. The move will cause great lamentation among we natives as the Owens family has been very popular with us all."

Refusing to believe the "cement was dry" on this deal—and leaning on his penchant for working a wrong long enough to make it right— Bill continued to try reaching the District Commander by phone—and finally got through, pleading his case for staying put.

"Sit tight," the commander said. "I'll get back to you."

All the Coast Guard units were on the same telephone line. When Bill heard the ring for the lifeboat station, he took the receiver down. "Leave Owens alone!" he heard the District Commander tell the lifeboat station officer. "I Repeat. Leave Owens alone!"

The officer was clearly trying to run Owens out of town—but it would only happen over the District Commander's dead body. Bill Owens was staying put, even if the incident angered him to no end.

Bill had worn a Coast Guard uniform during the war. "There was this one captain who gave me hell for being out of uniform because I didn't have a cap on. He came back the next year. In the meantime, the war had ended, and I went back to the Civil Service. I saw him stopping in front of my office and I happened to have my hat on. I started out, turned around, took off my hat, and threw it back into the house."

"Didn't you get reprimanded last year for being out of uniform?" the captain said.

"Yep."

"Why haven't you got a cap on now?"

"I don't belong to the Coast Guard anymore. I'm a civil servant. I don't have to."

Undoubtedly, Bill had an ornery streak to him. But when it came to the Coast Guard, Owens would seem to have earned that right.

Every few years, the light tower required painting. A difficult task at any station, painting was especially challenging at Arena with its tall tower. The process used was primitive by today's standards—and dangerous. A man would be lowered from the top of the lighthouse—in a barrel, which, with a sudden gust of wind, could be as vulnerable as a party balloon in front of a fan.

"Bill was the lightest weight of any of the men, so he was the one in the barrel until he became officer-in-charge," Isabel said.

The crew would lower Owens, dangling by a series of ropes, and rotate him around the tower. He would spend the day with a sprayer, suspended in air, painting the tower from top to bottom.

Owens was rarely seen without the pipe he smoked. But he had developed a habit of chewing tobacco when he was working outside, a habit Isabel didn't like. One day, after Bill's promotion to officer-in-charge, he had men high up on scaffolding painting the tower.

"Bill looked up," said Isabel, enjoying the memory, "and yelled something to the men. While he was yelling, he swallowed his cud of tobacco. That made him sick to his stomach; but it cured him of chewing tobacco!"

By 1949, the government began hiring contract painters to scaffold and paint the tower. Owens and his crew happily passed along the responsibility to the professionals.

Though not as dangerous as Conception's or Sur's, Point Arena's steep drop-offs still required caution. The steepest bluffs that surrounded the point were off-limits—Bill and Isabel had made that clear. And the Devil's Punch Bowl, just beyond the fog-signal toward the point, was never to be flirted with. It was far too dangerous.

Centuries of erosion had created a gaping sinkhole resembling a wide vortex. The sides were steep—with soil that easily collapsed beneath one's feet. When the tide was high or the ocean swells breaking with force, water charged in from one end, surged up the other side, then sucked out the bottom of the Punch Bowl's base—in a fast and turbulent boil.

Bill had read in the old records about a third assistant keeper who had walked to the edge of the blowhole. As the keeper peered over the edge, he lost his footing and fell. "They never did see him again," Owens said.

The family's second oldest, Sarah, had a touch of daredevil in her. Despite the severe cautions she had received, Sarah saw the Punch Bowl as a challenge that tempted her risky spirit from time to time.

"I had always been told that the Devil's Punch Bowl was very dangerous and that if you ever fell in you would never make it out," she said. "The waves would take you out to sea. But I felt that I could climb down at a low tide and get back out."

One day, she decided to test her theory. She climbed down, waited until the water sucked out, and hurriedly touched the bottom, then climbed back up. Triumphant!

"The children didn't tell me about the Punch Bowl until many years later," said Isabel. "When they did, I about fell off the chair."

Despite Sarah's successful—though foolish—venture down the blowhole, the surrounding bluffs posed a grave danger to anyone taking their presence lightly.

Several years later, the girls were playing at the base of a gentle slope

The Devil's Punch Bowl was located just beyond the fog-signal building toward the point.

down one bluff. The slope's trail was deceptive. Near the top, the path forked. To the left was the safe trail to the top. To the right, the path rounded a corner; just beyond hid a steep and dangerous drop. The children knew which fork to follow. Their dog, Pal, did not.

Jean has never forgotten seeing the dog charging up the bluff, then turning toward the drop-off, just past the curve. He plunged over the edge.

"Oh no!" the girls cried. "Pal! Pal!"

The sisters hurried to the edge and peered over to see if the dog had fallen onto rocks or sand—or into the ocean. Fifty feet below, Pal lay motionless on the sand. With the bluff too steep to descend, the children raced across the field to find their father.

Bill was talking with his crew when the children found him. One Coast Guardsman volunteered to help. Owens drove the Packard near the cliff, secured a rope to the back bumper and trussed the young crewman to the other end. He then lowered the sailor down by backing the car slowly toward the edge.

When the guardsman reached the sand, he secured Pal in a basket and Bill slowly moved the car forward until the dog was brought to the top. Owens then quickly repeated the process to retrieve the sailor.

Bill brought Pal to their home. There was no veterinarian in town and nothing more could be done for him but hope he could recover. But his injuries proved too severe and he died a few days later. Pal's loss reflected the thin line between safety and sorrow that stretched north and south on this rugged coastline: for sailors, for fishermen, for Coast Guardsman, and, at times, even for the pets of light keepers.

Pal was buried on the grounds at the light station.

It was a hard loss to swallow. As days passed, Isabel tried to help the children put the incident in perspective. She knew many thousands of American families had suffered losses of far greater magnitudes. In the end, only time eased the pain.

Bill Owens had been climbing the 145 steps to the lantern room at Point Arena for a decade. Inside the tower a spiral staircase led to the top. Every so often there was a landing for the keeper to catch his breath and a window to allow daylight to fill the magnificent stack. With Bill now in his late forties, the stairs were more challenging with each passing year. On Bill's hikes up the tower, his daughters often followed.

Jean would write, "When Joan and I were small, we would run up the stairs. We could never make it to the top without stopping. The fields, barns, and houses looked like miniatures the higher we climbed. As we got older, Dad taught us how to light the tower. He had already taught our older sisters and they'd accomplished the feat. I loved having the responsibility. I knew it was tiring for Dad to be up and down the tower so often."

On the weekends, visitors were allowed on the station and could go up the tower if they were accompanied by a crew member. If it was her father who happened to be on-watch, Diana would be right behind. "I'd be giving the facts about the tower to the visitors. I was probably accurate since I'd heard Dad describe everything so often. Some of the visitors may have thought I was a pest."

No visitors were allowed on the station during the war. But after the war, it seemed as though tourists were making up for lost time. "We had plenty come to the station," said Bill. "And they *all* wanted to go up the tower."

Though the war had ended, there was still frequent navy and army air maneuvers off the station. It was on July 14, 1947, that the Navy blimp *K-99* was headed north on a routine operational flight from Moffett Field, gliding directly toward the lighthouse at Point Arena.

"It was flying pretty low and the guys in there were waving at me," Bill Owens said. "I waved back. The blimp passed so low it scraped the side of the light tower."

Later that day, the blimp reached Cape Mendocino, where it suddenly dove from an altitude of 400 feet and splashed into the ocean a half-mile from shore. The crew flashed an S.O.S., boarded a rubber liferaft, and was rescued by a launch from the Blunt's Reef lightship.

The impact loosened the blimp's gondola. Freed from the weight of the gondola, eight-man crew, and three passengers, the blimp zoomed upward again and vanished inland. Two hours later, it struck a mountain near Eureka and collapsed.

With Bill and Isabel facing transfer threats and crashes of planes and LTAs, it was almost easy for them to miss noticing what was happening right in front of them: their three oldest girls had become young women.

The oldest, Shirley, married a young Coast Guardsman named Clifford Stormes. Their first home would be at the Point Arena Light Station, where Cliff was assigned under his new father-in-law, Bill Owens. Sarah followed the next year. She also married a Coast Guardsman, Jack Swartz. And in the summer of 1948, Dixie wed a third Coast Guard fellow, Richard Spence.

The new family members had known about the rift between the two service branches. And although they were Coast Guardsmen, they liked Bill and stood on his side. Bill would need all the support possible. Because in 1948, the Coast Guard attempted to replace him by assigning an enlisted man as the new officer-in-charge at the station.

"Some of the Coast Guard officers, they just had no use for lighthouses," Bill said emphatically. "Or for the old Lighthouse Service men, either."

Isabel agreed. "There was a man down at the District Office, an officer whose name was Bolin. He was head of personnel and he wanted to get rid of the old civilian lighthouse people."

When Cliff, the Owens' new son-in-law, was at the District Office to get his discharge, he had to go through the personnel office. While Cliff sat in Bolin's office, a young Guardsman entered and posted a chart listing each light station's officer-in-charge and the men serving under him. At the top of the Point Arena station was "William Owens."

But, apparently, not for long.

"When I get through here that name is going to be on the bottom," Cliff overheard Bolin say as he pointed to his father-in-law's name.

Unable to demote Bill without approval—and lots of red tape—from Washington, D.C., Bolin simply installed a new head keeper at Point Arena, giving the station two.

"So, there we were," said Isabel, "with two head keepers, and neither one would stand watches. The poor kids had to do it all."

Bolin's strategy was clear—and unfair. The *Mendocino Beacon* caught wind of the situation and published an article supportive of Owens in its February 14, 1948, edition.

"We hear a move is under way," wrote the *Beacon*, "to replace all the lighthouse keepers who have served so long and so well. When the Lighthouse Service was joined to the Coast Guard, the keepers were promised that no discrimination would be shown. But now come orders that the light keepers are to be replaced by enlisted men of the Coast Guard. This hardly seems fair … Owens has kept his station above standard, has never had any trouble with his men … and has treated the boys as part of his family." (In Bill's case, many of them actually were!)

For the second time in three years, the civil servant's position as light keeper had been threatened.

"When they sent that man in," Owens said, "their excuse was they had to have a military man. I got ahold of Congressman Miller and a State senator from Santa Rosa. They started shooting in letters to the Admiral in Washington. One day, [the admiral] got tired of all these letters and just pulled the man out. Sent him back to sea."

The Owens family, minus Shirley, gather in the living room circa 1947. Back left to right is Dixie, Sarah, Isabel, and Bill reclined on the couch. Front row, left is Joan, Jean, and Diana. (Courtesy of Owens family)

In the spring of that year, the Owens family received exciting—and stunning—news. Isabel, at age forty-four, was pregnant with another child. There was more: the Owens daughter, Shirley, was also pregnant with her and Cliff's second child. By chance, the babies were due at the same time. Bill and Isabel would seemingly have the rare joy of welcoming both their own child, and a grandchild, into the family—simultaneously.

Meanwhile, a fresh sense of optimism was sweeping across the station. The war was over, a war that had come on the heels of the Depression. Good times seemed to be returning. The sound of Joan and Diana practicing the piano wafted through the house, much to Bill and Isabel's delight.

In the Owens home, Diana, now nine, looked forward—for once! —to being an older sister. But during a check-up late in the pregnancy, the doctor could not hear a heartbeat. Isabel reported she had felt no recent movement. In the days that followed, the diagnosis became clear to both physician and parents: the baby would be stillborn.

Her doctor told Isabel she would need to proceed with the childbirth through normal delivery. Isabel and Shirley were admitted to the same small hospital, on the same November day. Shirley delivered her second child—a healthy daughter. Isabel delivered her last—without a heartbeat.

For the Owens family, it was a riptide from joy to sorrow that nobody could have imagined, an irony too sad to fathom. The two babies were born one day apart, Shirley's named Virginia and Isabel's named Susan.

Bill and Isabel's last baby was buried in the Odd Fellows Cemetery just outside Point Arena, beneath a headstone on which were etched the words, "Susan Owens. An angel lies here."

No one knew how to handle the loss. Neither Bill nor Isabel explained it. The girls intuitively knew what had happened. In an era when such devastating losses were often left unspoken, Bill and Isabel hid their grief, and carried on.

"They never mentioned it to us," said Diana, "and we didn't ask."

Keeper Owens on-watch at Point Arena. (Courtesy of Point Cabrillo Light Keepers Association)

Chapter Thirteen

The Pacific Enterprise

There was a time, early in the history of light stations, when the fog-signal was powered by steam. Wood was burned to heat water in boilers to produce a blast from the horn. The Point Arena station was known to burn 150 cords of wood a year for that sole purpose.

Now, in 1949, diesel engines could be instantly fired-up to provide power for the foghorn to belch forth its two-toned "bee-ooh." The tremendous bellow, however, sometimes reacted strangely in sea fog off Point Arena. At times, it could be heard clearly ten miles out to sea. But there were also areas where it seemed unable to penetrate the fog and the horn's blast couldn't be heard at all.

"I was down there one day," said Bill, "and I'd been running the foghorn. Hadn't shut it down all night. The next morning, the aids-to-navigation officer came on the station. He was standing right next to me, and the foghorn was a-runnin'. Just then, Isabel brought us a message: "'Captain Allen, the schooner *Lumbertown* is off Point Arena. He says the foghorn's not blowing.'"

The commander stared out to sea in amazement. He'd just learned firsthand how fog could sometimes silence the tremendous blast of the foghorn—and be unheard by sea captains.

Isabel handed the message to Bill—and Bill passed it to the commander.

"Here you are."

"I'll take care of that," he said to Bill.

Decades later, Bill said, "That's the only complaint I ever had against me about the light or foghorn. And he was wrong. But that's the way Point Arena is. There's a silent spot west of the light. Out there, they can't get the radio beacon and they can't get the foghorn either. And if it's foggy then the light's no good."

It was late August, a time when sea fog is most common along the California coast. Summer was in its final days. Jean, Joan, and Diana were savoring the last of their vacation and preparing to begin the new school year. And the station operated as it always did in uneventful stretches, in a sort of routine efficiency.

At the same time, in Vancouver, British Columbia, a man named Malcolm Cogle, a mariner from Harwich, England, was being celebrated. He was the captain of the *Pacific Enterprise*, a 454-foot freighter of the Furness-Withy Line. Cogle was about to begin his final voyage before retirement—the conclusion of a long and successful career of fifty-one years at sea. He was heading home—back to England—for good.

A front-page photo in the August 26, 1949, edition of *The Vancouver Daily Province* newspaper captured the excitement of the event. In the grainy photograph, Cogle is surrounded by fellow officers and crewmen of the *Pacific Enterprise*. The captain displays a radiant smile as he looks directly at the photographer. He is seated in an easy chair, with his legs outstretched and his feet resting upon a matching ottoman, gifts presented by the smiling crew and owners of the ship.

Described as "a sturdy man with twinkling blue eyes," Malcolm had been at sea dating back to his youth. His record was unblemished.

There were celebrations and luncheons scheduled at several

ports-of-call for the *Pacific Enterprise* during her return trip home to England. At each port, Cogle was to be honored.

The man was certainly deserving of such. In 1946, Cogle had been awarded the Order of the British Empire for his war service—when he'd shipped in the Atlantic and British Isles without a break for the six-year duration of the war. Another Vancouver paper reported that Cogle had operated on convoy duty between New York and London without a mishap, despite his ship being attacked several times. He had evaded German Luftwaffe aerial bombardments on numerous occasions in the Atlantic.

During a luncheon honoring Cogle that day in 1949, the crew cheered and sang, "For

Captain Malcolm Cogle of the **Pacific Enterprise** *sits in an easy-chair given to him in celebration of his final voyage before retirement. The photo appeared in the* **Vancouver Daily Province** *in late August 1949.*

He's a Jolly Good Fellow" to the popular captain. After the meal, Cogle toasted his ship and said, "May good luck and good weather continue to bless the *Pacific Enterprise* and all her crew." To celebrate the occasion, Furness-Withy employees were given a half-day holiday.

Cogle received a pen and pencil set "so he will have no excuse not to write his friends here," it was said.

The freighter had been built in Glasgow, Scotland, in 1928. Now, twenty-one years later, she was about to embark on yet another return trip to her home port of London. The *Pacific Enterprise* would, among others, make stops at Seattle and San Francisco. Upon reaching San Pedro, Los Angeles's harbor, the captain would again be honored, this time with a gold-watch ceremony commemorating his splendid career.

On August 31, the ship sailed from Vancouver. She left the wharf with a 9,300-ton cargo of wheat, lumber, zinc, lead, canned salmon, and flour. It was an easy passage to Puget Sound, where she loaded more lumber at the Washington cities of Tacoma, Olympia, and Everett. Her total now rose to 1.5 million board feet of lumber.

With the ship's cargo fastened, Cogle guided the *Pacific Enterprise* north from Tacoma, weaving up the Sound. Then he coursed westward through the Strait of San Juan De Fuca. The ship was now in open ocean. Here, the captain set a course south. The seas were mild; the vessel's compliment of fifty-four crew members and officers engaged in their familiar pattern of work shifts.

The ship had made four round-trip voyages per year between London and Vancouver with Cogle in command. This was considered a routine run.

Though she was a freighter, the vessel occasionally carried small numbers of passengers—as she did on this voyage. The five tourists had the pleasure of their staterooms, dining, and smoking salons. There were Mr. and Mrs. Hennicker of Vancouver Island, bound for Los Angeles, and C.H. Bockie of Edinburgh. Others booked for the journey to England were Dorothy Skelton of Essex, England, and John Matthews of Oakland, California, who planned to continue his university studies in the United Kingdom.

In 1949, the tools for finding one's way at sea were still, for most ships, very basic. The use of maps, charts, clocks, and compasses were standard. Freighters used celestial navigation with sextants to measure the angle between the stars, moon, or sun, and the horizon. Better equipped vessel had radio receivers for directional assistance from radio beacons. But with every method, if a navigator misidentified his markers, he could take the ship dangerously off course. And bad weather could make such navigation even more challenging.

As the *Pacific Enterprise* steamed south over the next few days, the weather began to slowly worsen. Wispy threads of fog would appear and then disperse. No one was alarmed; the ship was safely offshore. But soon fog arrived again—and began to thicken. Visibility, which had been five miles, decreased rapidly. Three miles, two miles, and now, by sunset on Thursday, September 8, visibility in the fog could be measured by literal yards.

Still, the ship's officers and passengers were confident the vessel was safely twenty miles offshore.

At sunrise on Friday, September 9, the fog-shrouded ship was mired in a soup so thick the bow was barely visible to the officers on the bridge. With the *Pacific Enterprise* at already-reduced speed, Captain Cogle ordered his first officer to slow the ship further and begin blowing for fog, her horn emitting a blast every minute.

It was 9 A.M. Passengers were having breakfast in the salon. At the Point Arena Light Station, Bill Owens was also having breakfast. He was seated at the kitchen table. Isabel was washing dishes. Bill could hear the station's booming two-tone fog-signal blast. It had been blowing throughout the night.

Then, Bill heard something else: a second horn of a different pitch. The sound was coming from the ocean. With each blast, the ship's horn sounded closer and closer. His knuckles tapped the table. He glanced toward the ocean—and glanced yet again.

"That ship's too close!" he yelled as he bolted out the door and into the fog.

The officers aboard the *Pacific Enterprise*, still believing the vessel was clear of any danger, were shocked when they suddenly heard the loud blare of the Point Arena fog-signal. Thinking it was a horn-blast from another ship, Cogle ordered, "Hard right!" It took time for the vessel to respond, but the *Pacific Enterprise* slowly began to swing to starboard. In the confusion of the moment, Cogle was unsure of his position.

Bill and Isabel both knew. The ship was in grave danger. Bill hadn't reached the tower before he heard the grating screech from the *Enterprise's* hull.

She let out a long and sustained distress blast—a ship's signal that could mean only one of two things: the vessel had run aground or collided with another craft. Bill could not yet see the ship, but he suspected what proved to be true: It had hit Arena Rock, about a mile off the west end of the light station.

The ship was wedged hard into the notorious reef that covered nearly one-and one-half acres below the water's surface. For a brief moment, the officers on the bridge stood motionless as they tried to regroup and assess what had happened. Their worst nightmare had just become reality.

The freighter now sat upright on the reef, as stable as a parked car. The seas were gentle, for now. In a scene of irony, the fog began to slowly lift. Cogle tried to reverse the engines and back the vessel off, but the effort proved fruitless.

On shore, Bill immediately called the lifeboat station. A motorized launch was dispatched and soon arrived off the light station to remove passengers. Several Coast Guard sailors boarded the ship by ladder.

"All passengers will leave the ship with us now," the Guardsmen insisted.

Since the sea was calm, so were the passengers. But the Guardsmen knew the ocean may not remain calm; and if it didn't, neither would the passengers. The five guests of the ship donned life jackets and carefully descended by ladder to the lifeboat. Guardsmen lowered their suitcases by rope.

Though the few travelers were now safely on the small-motor launch, the captain and crew were initially allowed to stay aboard. For Cogle, the faint hope of his ship surviving twitched on and off like a lamp cord shorting out. Perhaps, he thought, she could be lifted by a high tide and pulled free when the big Coast Guard cutters arrived on the scene.

But the life of the *Pacific Enterprise* was slipping away—doomed by Arena Rock—something even the Nazis hadn't been able to accomplish with a Cogle-commanded ship.

"They didn't want to leave the ship," Bill said. "But the Coast Guard told them, 'It's goin' down. We're gonna take you off.'"

The Coast Guard ran up the Black Ball flag, meaning the ship was not abandoned and, thus, off limits for salvagers. The next day, the ocean swells grew larger. Cogle and his crew accepted the inevitable. They climbed down rope ladders and off the ship to the waiting rescue crafts.

A reporter from the *Mendocino Beacon* described the crew and officers as the obvious—depressed. "They stood solidly behind their skipper," he wrote, "and when asked just what had happened, to a man they

The San Francisco Call *newspaper ran this photo of the* Pacific Enterprise, *impaled upon Arena Rock, before she sank off Point Arena in September 1949. (Courtesy of San Francisco Maritime Museum)*

exclaimed, "'Twas an act of God.'"

Captain Cogle and his crew were taken to San Francisco where arrangements for their passage home were made.

Bill never believed the *Pacific Enterprise* could be freed from Arena Rock. He was right.

As word of the wreck spread among the locals, increasing numbers flocked to the station. Among them were friends of Bill and Isabel, farmers from Colusa who were arriving for a scheduled visit with the Owens family. They had brought boxes of peaches and placed them on the porch. It was a far as they could get; Isabel was waxing floors inside.

Diana, now ten, saw the boxes on the porch, then glanced at the hordes of sightseers walking past the house toward the bluffs. Almost simultaneously, the youngster loaded up a bag with the gifted fruit, stood at the front gate, and sold the peaches to passersby for a dime a piece. "I was lucky that Mom and Dad had a sense of humor."

Newsmen swarmed the light station like locusts.

Even keeping the station gate closed proved useless. People parked their cars, jumped the fence, or walked around the gate. The news crews filmed the action.

"It was exciting," said Joan, "when the film was shown at our little the-ater in Point Arena. Dad was pictured being interviewed by the report-ers and you couldn't help feeling like a celebrity."

For three days a steady stream of cars came and went from the light-house. Cameras clicked all day long and every other person was carrying binoculars or a spyglass of some description. Bill and his crew had their hands full keeping people away from the bluff's edge. "But," wrote the *Beacon*, "light keeper Wm. Owens and his crew were cordial and cour-teous to all."

The *Enterprise* had shifted by now and was sitting on the reef headed to sea. But she was settling. As the seas increased, waves began breaking over her aft end. Soon, the wheat in the ship's holds swelled to the break-ing point. The bulkheads of the *Enterprise* split. Her contents began to spill into the sea and drift slowly to the beaches: lumber, cans of salmon, 100-pound sacks of flour, and more.

By Monday morning, the stern was under water. Though the ship, nor its cargo, had been abandoned, "the native pirates and beachcomb-ers are anxiously awaiting the drift to start floating in," wrote the *Beacon*.

The ship finally split in two as the waves, and swelling wheat within her holds, caused her hull to burst. The stern went first and, a few days later, the forward, both resting in sixty feet of water.

After the ship broke apart up, cargo began to wash ashore. Bill had to close the station. People were driving in with trucks, hoping to load up with the merchandise. This, of course, was illegal. The cargo belonged to the company that bought the salvage rights. But that didn't stop the poachers.

Hundreds of flour sacks washed ashore. Oddly, much of it was still useable. The flour had an inch of crust on it from the sea water. Inside that, it was dry. A small rug from the ship floated in, too. A Coast Guardsman found it. He intended to use it as a floor mat for his car. Isa-bel wanted to save it. "So, I offered him $5 for it and he accepted."

The Coast Guard had sent several large cutters up from San Fran-cisco to rescue the officers and crew. At the time the vessels began rac-ing toward Point Arena, there remained the slim possibility the freighter could be towed off the reef. One of the cutters was the 310-foot *Gresham*; aboard the ship was a young sailor named Ed Carpenter.

Soon thereafter, Carpenter received his transfer papers to report for duty at Point Arena Light Station. There, he was to be under the direct command of Bill Owens, who would one day become his father-in-law.

———————

By the end of the decade, the twins had turned seventeen. When one of them, Jean, passed Ed at the light station, they began chatting. Gradually, they both realized how much they enjoyed the encounters. Apparently, Bill noticed, too.

Ed was standing watch one evening in the fog-signal building. Jean noticed her mother had gone into town and her father was sound asleep on the couch. Conditions for a quick visit with Ed, she realized, were ideal.

"It was dark and slightly foggy. I decided to take the path near the bluffs so no one would see me since we were not allowed at the signal room."

After navigating the precarious trail along the bluff's edge, and being foolhardy, she thought, in walking the bluff at night, she arrived. "As I opened the door, I could not believe my eyes. There was my dad standing in the room—right next to Ed. How he knew what I was up to is beyond me."

Like her twin sister, Joan had developed an interest in a young Coast Guardsman, this one Don Silva. He was assigned to the lifeboat station about seven miles from the lighthouse. Too far apart for "conversations in passing," both realized another method of communication was needed: a note exchange through the officer-in-charge's mail run.

"Guess who was the carrier?" Diana asked rhetorically.

When Joan had a note to send Don, she made sure Diana joined her father on the mail run. That was fine with Diana. To her, the weekend rides in the Coast Guard truck with her father were a treat. The two would drive down Main Street, stop at the post office, then continued until turning right on Port Road. One mile further and they'd reach the lifeboat station at the cove.

Bill would walk into the office, chat with the men, and deliver their posts. As soon as Bill was through the front door, Don was poised and ready. He'd walk briskly to the passenger side of the truck, get his note, place his return message in Diana's hand, and skedaddle. "When I think of it all now," she said smiling, "I'm certain Dad was not fooled."

Riding the mail run together was a treat for Bill, too; he rarely had time alone with one of his girls, but when he did, he relished it.

There were only three daughters at home now; three were married and gone. The workload for Isabel was less demanding. There was more time for the children, and occasionally, a chance to create a memory.

"At night, after dishes were done, Mom and I would go for a walk up the road," Diana warmly recalled. "There was a large cattle ranch bordering the station and we could hear the cattle moving on one side of us and the sea lions and ocean on the other. Being out in the country, there were no lights except for the beam of the light tower that would sweep across our path every few seconds. Mom would point out all the constellations to me on those walks. With the air so clear, they were easy to see."

The *Pacific Enterprise* was only one of several freighters that gave North Coast residents a close look at big ships during Bill's time at Point Arena. Another large freighter became the subject of a wreck with a decidedly happier ending—the *Kenkoku Maru*.

When Shigeo Fujimi, captain of the 7,000-ton vessel, steamed out of Nagoya, Japan, he plotted a course for the Golden Gate. He missed his target by eighty miles.

It was 1 A.M. on April 28, 1951, when a young Coast Guardsman on duty at the Point Arena light said he'd heard a vessel heading south—wildly blowing its whistle in a rainstorm. Twenty miles further down the coast, the *Kenkoku Maru* left the rain behind only to enter a dense fog. The captain, under the impression he was drawing near the Golden Gate, ordered his helmsman to turn to port, a left swing he thought would take the ship to San Francisco Bay. He was startled by the gut-wrenching

The Japanese freighter, **Kenkoku Maru**, *stranded on a shallow reef near present day Sea Ranch.*

sound of rocks tearing into his hull. Fujimi had steered his ship straight into a cove just north of Black Point—near present day Sea Ranch.

Still thinking he was aimed for San Francisco Bay, Fujimi now reasoned he must have hit the Farallon Islands. When the sun came up and the fog had thinned, he realized he'd hit the coast.

"That morning," Bill said, "there was a Japanese crew member standing out on the highway with a sign: 'Call Coast Guard.'"

Large crowds gathered on the headlands to monitor the ship's fate. She was resting on a shallow reef—an ugly mass of black basalt that jutted 100 yards into the sea—and so close to the beach that at low tide her crew could walk to dry sand. Her double-bottom hull had ruptured on the rocks; seven feet of water flooded the engine room.

Salvage engineers estimated they had a fifty-fifty chance of saving the ship and determined the best—and perhaps only—chance to free the vessel was to pull her off on one of the year's highest tides—just three weeks away. On the evening of May 22, an offshore derrick barge, beach crews, and tugs simultaneously took up the strain. Within a half-hour, the ship began to quiver. Soon, the stern swung slowly out toward sea. When she was floated to freedom, one-hundred observers on the beach exploded with cheers. The *Kenkoku Maru* (meaning "heavenly country") was successfully towed to Alameda for extensive repairs.

"The ship was lucky," said Bill, "because the waves weren't big."

"'Call Coast Guard,'" he said again, with a wry chuckle.

Several months later, the Owens family had two events to cheer instead of lament. On September 16, 1951, at the Point Arena Methodist Church, Joan married Don Silva. Two weeks later, Jean married Ed Carpenter. As the excitement of the weddings and celebrations passed, and life returned to normal, a stark reality hit. The Owens home was down to only one child, twelve- year-old Diana—and the house seemed empty.

Bill was fifty-one years old. It was time, he and Isabel believed, to consider transferring to another light. A fresh station. A new dwelling. But nothing, they knew, could replace Point Arena as home.

There was soon to be an opening just up the coast. Point Cabrillo Light Station needed a new officer-in-charge. The lighthouse tower was short. And, according to the previous keeper, Cabrillo was "one of the prettiest light stations between San Luis Obispo and the Oregon border."

Bill put in for the job. He had plenty of seniority. The District Office in San Francisco, now the 12th District under the Coast Guard, approved the transfer. Owens was to report for duty in January 1952.

He accepted the transfer—under one condition. The Coast Guard had to move the government piano, or "pie-anna" as Bill called it, up to Cabrillo. They agreed.

The Coast Guard may have considered it an unusual—even trivial—request. But the piano was anything but trivial to the Owens family—and to Bill in particular. Two of his daughters, Joan and Diana, had taken piano lessons for years and Bill delighted in hearing them play. Often, the girls sat at the keyboard, fingers gliding back-and-forth, while their father relaxed on the couch, with curling ribbons of smoke rising from his pipe. His favorite song was a popular tune of the '40s called "Till the End of Time." Both girls learned the tune by heart. "We played it for him whenever he wanted to hear it," Diana said.

Five daughters were now married. The family's era at the lighthouse

Joan Owens and Don Silva are flanked by Bill and Isabel on their wedding day in September 1951. Isabel made Joan's wedding dress—as well as the dress of Joan's twin sister Jean, who was married two weeks later. (Courtesy of Owens Family)

was ending—but never to be forgotten. The following spring, the fields behind their house at the light station would, once again, be covered by wildflowers with their brilliant blues, yellows, and pinks. In the years to come, the girls' memories would often take them back to Point Arena, where the fields were always a magnificent, flowered tapestry, and the sweetest strawberries grew.

Part V

Chapter Fourteen

Cabrillo

The day the Owens family left Point Arena—January 22, 1952—was Isabel's forty-eighth birthday. They drove the narrow two-lane State Route 1 north along the coast. The highway crossed Big River at the picturesque village of Mendocino—soon to be discovered by Hollywood—then passed through the small lumber town of Caspar. In between, if one looked carefully, a sign could be seen on the ocean side of the highway, nearly hidden by a lane of trees. It marked Lighthouse Road and the entry to Point Cabrillo Light Station.

The one-lane road descended gently in an arrow-straight line through the neighboring ranchlands before reaching the lighthouse reservation gate. Just beyond stood a row of Cypress trees. The roadway veered gently left, and then to the right. The Owens car slowly rolled forward to the family's new home. To their right, three lovely cottages appeared—each two-story—and lined by a gleaming white picket fence. Two-hundred yards further ahead stood the lighthouse on the point, looking more like

Point Cabrillo Light Station, located two miles north of Mendocino, as it appeared during Bill Owens' tenure at the station. The Owens home is at the far right. (Courtesy of Point Cabrillo Light Keepers Association)

a stately country church.

The move to Point Cabrillo had been a small one in distance—only thirty-five miles—but it was titanic in emotion. The family's "coming-of-age" years were rooted in Point Arena; whether joy (the girls falling in love), angst (the Coast Guard-civilian tension), fear (the threat of Japanese invasion during World War II) or loss (the stillborn baby), hundreds of memories had been made there. Summer vacations. School and studies. Christmas and New Year's. Graduations and marriages. The birth of the first Owens grandchildren.

Home at Cabrillo would be different; once a brood of eight, only Bill, Isabel, and Diana would live at the new site. Diana was apprehensive about the move. "We loaded up everything and left a home and area I loved. I couldn't imagine anyone else living in our home."

The transfer also marked a different stage of Bill's career. Every previous move—Conception, Sur, and Arena—had been filled with anticipation of the future. But now, Owens was entering the twilight of his working years. Bill had reached his early fifties. The steps to climb to the Point Arena lantern room had become excessively taxing. Isabel and the six girls all believed Bill needed a less demanding station. A shorter light tower. A smaller crew to manage.

Bill saw the move differently. "The reason they transferred me to Cabrillo was I got along good with the fellas. They were having a lot of trouble up there and they sent me up to straighten the station out."

The family could not have asked for a more suitable setting. The lighthouse reservation was within a few miles of both Mendocino and Fort Bragg. All the services they'd need—groceries, banking, hardware, and schools—were close by. The light itself was only thirty-two feet above the ground, a fifth the height of the Point Arena tower. The lantern room required only the climb of two short—albeit steep—ship's ladders.

The family moved into the middle cottage. With no sisters at home, Diana had her choice of bedrooms. She chose the room facing west to the light tower so she could have the light flash through her window every ten seconds. While the "strobe effect" might be intolerable to most, such was not the case for the youngest Owens. "It was comforting," she said.

This 1952 aerial photo shows the narrow strip of land leading to the lighthouse on the right. The three keeper dwellings are visible between the rows of trees. (Courtesy of Point Cabrillo Light Keepers Association)

As weeks passed, the Owens family made the necessary adjustments. Bill became familiar with his new crew. With the arrival of spring, Isabel planted her garden. And Diana—entering seventh grade mid-year—began to make new friends at school in Mendocino. Plus, there were spectacular caves and beaches to be explored.

"Still, it was lonely at first without Jean and Joan."

The U.S. Geological Survey named the point in 1870 after the discoverer of California, Portuguese explorer Juan Rodriquez Cabrillo. Old-timers from the area pronounce the name "Cuh-brill-oh," utilizing the Portuguese enunciation. More recently, people have used the Spanish pronunciation of "Cuh-bree-oh." The correct manner depends on Cabrillo's ancestry. For centuries, Juan Rodriquez's nationality has been debated. One 17th-century Spanish historian identified the explorer as Portuguese. Others believe he may have been Spanish. Bill, Isabel, and their family always employed the Portuguese pronunciation.

The point's location had caught the attention of the United States Lighthouse Board as a potential site for a light station in the latter part of the 1800s.

A half-mile north of Cabrillo Point was a tea-cupped indentation along the headlands called Frolic Cove. It was there, in 1850, that the two-masted merchant ship *Frolic* ran aground on a submerged reef. The ship had been involved in the opium trade from the Orient, which was legal at the time. On this voyage, the *Frolic* was enroute to San Francisco from China and carrying 135 tons of cargo intended for sale in Gold Rush San Francisco. The ship was loaded with ceramics, wooden trunks, Chinese silks, furniture, and flatware—even a small, prefabricated house.

The *Frolic's* captain, Edward Faucon, was unfamiliar with the coast north of San Francisco and was using outdated maps. When rough seas struck as the ship approached the coast, she was slammed onto rocks by large swells.

No lives were lost in the wreck. But everything that could be salvaged of the *Frolic's* cargo was quickly gathered up by the local Pomo Indians. The rest was claimed by the sea. Insurance agents who came north from San Francisco to inspect the wreck soon determined nothing of worth remained. But during their site-examination, inspectors discovered far greater riches—the abundant coastal redwoods in the nearby forests. Soon after, the lumber industry prepared to capitalize on the valuable timber, began to established mills, and build the towns of Fort Bragg, Caspar, and Mendocino.

An extreme high demand for the redwoods developed after the 1906 earthquake and fire that destroyed San Francisco. The lumber was desperately needed to rebuild the city. And redwoods were available by the millions along California's North Coast.

The past loss of coastal merchant ships, and the commercial importance of the redwoods, convinced the government a lighthouse was needed to safeguard shipping and the delivery of products essential for the development of the region.

Local curiosity spiked at the time government surveys were made as to where the light would be located. Point Cabrillo was chosen as the new home for the beacon.

Twenty-three acres of land were initially purchased from a local farmer named David Gordon for that purpose. Ultimately, 30.5 acres would be sold to the government for the light station.

By September 1908, work on the lighthouse buildings was progressing nicely. A reporter from the *Mendocino Beacon* received a tour of the site from M.J. Wiley, the government engineer and project inspector. On September 19, 1908, the reporter wrote:

> The site selected is most beautiful. The ground is practically level, there being just enough slope to ensure good drainage. The point of land is about fifty feet above mean tide water and projects into the seas far enough to afford a good view of the coastline both ways. The light and fog-station building [are] well advanced and will be practically finished in two to three weeks and ready to receive the light and fog-signal apparatus.

The cliffs were nearly vertical and rose fifty feet above the surf. Numerous low rocks extended offshore, like roots of a tree, for more than two-hundred yards.

By the finish of construction, the station consisted of the lighthouse, three keeper's dwellings, storage buildings for each cottage, an oil house, a blacksmith/carpentry shop, and a water tower. Just south of the dwellings were a utility building and barn.

The Craftsman-style houses were located 600 feet east of the tower, each of the two-story dwellings provided ample space for families.

A phone system connected the watch room at the light with the keepers at all three residences. All station buildings were painted in the standard Lighthouse Service arrangement: cream color exterior with light brown trim and a red roof.

On June 10, 1909, the light at Point Cabrillo was activated for the first time.

The light tower featured, of course, a Fresnel lens. The gleaming third-order gem would magnify the light source into a beam visible fifteen miles out to sea. The lantern room was barely larger than the lens itself. Little more than a foot of space separated the keeper from the rotating optic.

The lens was mounted on ball bearings in raceway track, the slow spin powered by a drop-weight. Later, a small electric motor was installed to turn it.

The machinery for the foghorn was installed in the lower room of the light tower with "trumpets" placed facing seaward on the roof of the building.

"Mr. Wiley assures us [the foghorn] will make plenty of noise, even at Mendocino," said the newspaper.

The accuracy of the engineer's word was in question for only a short time. Tests of the foghorn soon confirmed its effectiveness. The *Mendocino Beacon* wrote the device "shows every indication of being able to awaken the dead."

The foghorn could be heard far across the landscape, as well at sea. A stage driver by the name of Jackson heard the signal while at Albion—a full ten-miles distant. He mistook it for a rancher's bellowing bull and said all the way up the coast that he was on the lookout for trouble.

The short tower stood only eighty-four feet above the ocean surface. The long stretch of unprotected coastline here, given the low elevation

This 1909 photo of the Point Cabrillo Light Station displays the light and fog-signal building, the blacksmith and carpentry shop and keepers dwelling in the distance.

of the light tower, required a high intensity light source to be seen at an adequate distance. By the time Owens transferred to Cabrillo in 1952, the station was using a one-thousand-watt bulb. The lens magnified the light to 1.1 million candlepower.

————

By early 1952, when the Owens family arrived, the world had suffered through two world wars and a devastating depression. The "atomic age" had begun. The Soviets had successfully detonated an atomic device in August 1949. With the geo-political tensions existing between the United States and the U.S.S.R., the "Cold War," as it was called, worsened overnight.

But like most other Americans, Bill and Isabel focused on the tasks of work, family, and school, and kept meeting their responsibilities. The family, which already had a cat, soon acquired another stray dog. A white mutt, part Terrier and part Cocker Spaniel, who had been roaming the station, found his way to the Owens home. Where he appeared from, no one knew. But they named him "Pug" and he quickly became Diana's inseparable friend.

The amiable dog seemed to relate to everyone. "Pug and our cat were so friendly they slept together in the same box," Isabel said.

Wild blackberries grew on the reservation, both in the field and in the Owens back yard. Pug often followed Isabel and Diana to the garden, where he loved to eat berries that grew there. "The dog got more berries than we ever did," Diana said.

On school days, Diana caught the school bus at the end of the lane. It was about a mile from home to the bus stop at the highway. Most days, she walked. But if the weather was poor, Bill would drive her to the stop in the morning—and be waiting for her in the afternoon.

One of the station's Coast Guardsmen became acquainted with a local rancher who agreed to pasture two of his horses at the station. Diana was ecstatic—the rancher let her ride any time she wanted on his acres and acres of land.

Isabel loved her garden. "We had gophers here, too, but not near as many as at Point Arena."

Pug, with his love for berries, wasn't the only animal that was a threat to her garden. A goat from a neighboring ranch had also discovered the garden. He'd jump the fence and make his way to the land-of-plenty. Once there, he ate everything in sight until one of the men would come and toss him back over the fence. The goat was undeterred. He returned time and again. Not just to Isabel's garden. Everyone's. The men finally had had enough. Frustrated at the loss of food meant for their table, they shot the goat in the leg and placed him on the other side of the fence. This time, they hoped, for good. The goat recovered and within a week began to walk. But never again did he jump the fence.

When the fog came in—which it did frequently—the horn would be activated. According to the *Pacific Coast Pilot*, the moody tones of the fog-signal could be heard during summer an average of 150 hours per month at Cabrillo.

The blast from the foghorn was an annoyance to many who lived nearby. The irascible Bill, of course, had little patience for such reactions.

"Right after I left [Point Cabrillo], some guy from the city bought an acre of land just off the light station and built a house there. He sued the Coast Guard because the foghorn kept him awake. The Lieutenant was telling me about it. I said it's a good thing I'm not there yet or I'd tell him, 'By God, this foghorn's been here since 1908. You come up here and bought the place right next to it and now you're kickin' about it!' Oh, I had people call me up from Fort Bragg. 'Can't you cut that foghorn off? It's keeping me awake.' That was when Noyo Harbor had a foghorn on the end of the jetty."

Isabel and Diana had no quarrels with the fog-signal's 'two-toned' wail. "Nothing put me to sleep faster than the sound of the foghorn," said Diana. Isabel agreed. "You get used to it," she said. "If it was shut off during the night, the silence would wake you up."

Diana and Pug were constant companions at the light station. The fog-signal building and tower are behind. Note the foghorn's trumpets on the roof. (Courtesy of Point Cabrillo Light Keepers Association)

Other annoyances bothered lighthouse neighbors. At some light stations, the beacon shined into bedrooms as the light pulsed or rotated. To maintain peace with the locals, keepers often painted the glass on the land side of the gallery.

Keeping the peace wasn't always easy. At times, it could be a challenge at one's own light station.

Upon first taking his new command at Cabrillo, Bill met with his crew. He knew exactly how he wanted the station to run, and he expected compliance. "If any of you don't like it, just let me know. You'll be transferred.'"

Soon, Bill discovered someone didn't like it. One Coast Guardsmen found it difficult to take orders and direction from a civilian supervisor. Bill listened to his grievance. But once it was clear the crewman had no intention of adapting to Bill as his officer-in-charge, Bill called the District Office and the Guardsman was transferred to a military facility. The station would run Bill's way. Period.

Within a short time, life again had found a harmonious flow. Bill's work as officer-in-charge included making watch assignments for each keeper. Around-the-clock watches, divided into six-hour shifts, were maintained at the station during the 1950s. Bill oversaw the operation and upkeep of the station as well as the local aids-to-navigation at Mendocino Bay and, nine miles to the north, Noyo Harbor. Both had buoys to be monitored, which Bill could easily accomplish with a simple drive-by visual check.

———

Noyo River, whose headwaters are in the Mendocino Range, winds its way to the ocean and concludes with several sharp S-curves as it reaches the Pacific. The fishing harbor lies sheltered behind one of the bends—only a short distance from the mouth of the river at the south end of Fort Bragg. A jetty protects the north side of the channel entrance. Bill was tasked with checking the automated foghorn on the jetty.

He made several trips a week to the harbor to check the horn and lights. Back at the station, he'd get his crew working, cutting grass, painting, and cleaning. Of course, they all had watches to stand, including Bill.

The young Coast Guardsmen were often new enlistees. And Bill had to train each their responsibilities—serious ones when it came to the light and foghorn.

"When you've got a bunch of eighteen-year-old kids, you've got to keep right behind them the whole way. Every now and then, they'd be on-watch and I'd hear a boat blowing out at sea. I'd jump out of bed, get down to the light. 'Why isn't this foghorn going?' They'd be asleep. It didn't happen very often. But if you fell asleep on me while you were on-watch, you were in trouble."

Buoys at Mendocino Bay had to be checked to ensure they were lit at night. It was Bill's job to monitor those, too. They were called A.G.A. lights and were lit by acetylene gas. Coast Guard boats from Fort Bragg would service the buoys monthly and replace the gas tanks.

In December 1953, Owens was inspecting Noyo with a group of Coast Guard officials. As they reached the harbor entrance, the party had a surprise waiting for them. The auxiliary foghorn on the jetty was missing. The *Press Democrat* in Santa Rosa ran the story's headline: "Who Stole the Foghorn at Fort Bragg?"

The Mendocino County Sheriff's Office and the Coast Guard officials were both stumped. Neither could determine the reason for the theft since the foghorn required too high a voltage to be used on boats; nor could it be sold if taken by pranksters. The case was never solved.

At Cabrillo, among Bill's many daily chores was a morning visit to nearby Fort Bragg. He was still the mailman for the station. The road Bill traveled from the entry of the light station to Fort Bragg was called the Shoreline Highway. The thin, two-lane road weaved its way through the trees and rolling coastal slopes of Caspar. It was a lovely drive. Few places along the coast were more beautiful.

As the road reached Caspar Beach, it crossed diminutive Doyle Creek where it became tightly pinched at the bridge. In January 1954, Bill was returning from Fort Bragg when the driver of a truck in the oncoming lane lost control on the soft shoulder. The truck swerved in front of the Coast Guard pick-up.

A stunned Bill watched the truck crash through the railing directly in front of him. Bill jammed on the brakes, swerved, and skidded to a stop just short of the wreckage. The truck cab had slid into the creek while the trailer remained lodged on the bridge—its driver pinned below against the cab's steering wheel.

Bill jumped out and scampered down the embankment and waded into the creek until he reached the truck. He opened the truck door, grabbed the driver—no seatbelts back then—and pulled him to safety.

Though the *Press Democrat* in Santa Rosa credited him with the rescue, Bill himself never bothered to mention it.

Point Cabrillo light tower and fog-signal building. (Author photo)

As the Cold War escalated between the United States and the U.S.S.R., a Civil Defense effort across America was put into place. The U.S. government set the goal of having all of America's observation posts manned round the clock.

Volunteers would watch for planes day and night. Charts were provided with images of Soviet and American planes at each post with directions to report all aircraft sighted.

In October 1953, Bill announced that a twenty-four-hour watch would be maintained at the light station by Civil Defense volunteers as part of Operation Skywatch.

While the Air Force oversaw operations, it was the responsibility of the post supervisor to recruit and train all volunteers at their post. Bill was the supervisor and chief observer for Point Cabrillo.

Men at the station took part in the observations, each crewmen averaging nearly twenty-five hours per month of off-duty volunteer assistance. A year later, Bill and his crew were awarded special merit pins for

250 hours [each] of Skywatch service.

Despite the high tension between nations, nothing ever came of the threat from enemy aircraft. In 1958 the program was ended nationwide.

Chapter Fifteen

Leaving the Light

During holidays, the Owens home became the gathering spot for as many family members as could make it. By the late 1950s, Bill and Isabel's brood had quickly ballooned to thirteen grandchildren. Visits usually lasted one to three nights—and Bill and Isabel loved them. Easter egg hunts, picnics, Thanksgiving feasts, and Christmas gift exchanges—the family jumped into all with both feet.

Meanwhile, Diana Owens became a teenager. Along with that milestone came the natural inclination for the companionship of her peers. But while Diana had developed a cadre of school friends, she didn't have the option of lengthy telephone chats like those enjoyed by her classmates.

"The one major drawback of being a teenager at Point Cabrillo was the telephone system," she remembered. "The Coast Guard had it set up so that every phone call, in or out, was an extra charge. So, if I called a friend, or one called me, Dad was charged for it."

Bill and Isabel relax in the living room. Throughout their time at Point Cabrillo, family gatherings happened right here. (Courtesy of Owens Family)

As Diana approached dating age, her parents maintained an appropriate level of supervision of their last child. Still, little appeared to escape her father's attention; Bill seemed to have eyes everywhere, as a young Mendocino boy named Joseph Brown soon found out.

A relationship between Diana and Joe, classmates at Mendocino High, was developing; Joe had already made several visits to see Diana at the light station.

"I was in tenth grade," Brown recalled. "I had just got my driver's license."

One day, Joe and three of his friends were driving his 1948 Chevy four-door through the streets of Mendocino. "Let's drive up the sidewalk on Main Street," said one of Joe's friends. "We can make it all the way up the block. And we can turn off at Doc Whited's driveway."

After a moment of consideration, everyone agreed, teeming with that seemed-like-a-good-idea-at-the-time mentality that distinguishes teenagers of any generation.

"I drove the car up on the sidewalk and was passing stores. As we went by Dick's Place (a local watering hole), Dick was sitting by the window. The first thing out of my mouth was, 'Oh god. I hope he didn't see me and tell Mr. Owens.'"

The next day, Joe drove to Point Cabrillo to see Diana. Bill was waiting for him; he had, indeed, heard from his friend Dick.

"He waved 'the holy finger' at me," Joe later said.

Bill paused long enough for his penetrating gaze to have the desired effect, then said, "Don't you know someone could have stepped out of a storefront and been hurt! Don't ever let me hear of you doing something like that again."

"And I never did," said Joe.

The admonition from Bill made a positive impact on the sixteen-year-old. Joe was determined not to disappoint the man again, an honorable inclination that Bill and Isabel apparently appreciated. Shortly afterward, they gave him permission to date their daughter.

"It was the first time I'd been allowed to go anywhere alone in a car with a date," remembered Diana.

The first-date evening went well and upon their return to the light station, Joe and Diana decided to ride down to the tower, turn around, and come back up to the house. The tower sat on a peninsula with ocean on three sides and steep drop-offs in all three directions. The foghorn, which had just been started, suddenly went off as Joe reached the light. The blast startled him so badly he let go of the wheel and the car headed for the bluff.

Joe's senses snapped back just in time; he slammed on the brakes short of the bluff. He and Diana looked at each other—wide-eyed. Now that they'd stopped, the specter of "Diana's Dad" lurked, at least in Joe's head.

"The first thing that went through Joe's mind was that Dad had come up behind him and was ready to do something to him," Diana recalled with a smile.

Nope. Neither Bill nor Isabel had noticed their wild adventure. The story would be shared years later—with much humor—after Joe had become the couple's sixth son-in-law.

Joe would eventually join the Navy, meaning all six Owens

Bill Owens, in dress uniform, at Point Cabrillo. (Courtesy of Point Cabrillo Light Keepers Association)

sons-in-law were either Coast Guard or Navy.

"Bill was proud of that," said Isabel.

At times, Coast Guard men who served under Bill at Point Arena and Point Cabrillo stations would come back to see him and talk over old times, Isabel said. "That meant a lot to him, too."

The gate to the lighthouse reservation was little more than a half-mile from Shoreline Highway. The station itself, with its lovely pastures, coves, and ocean views, was a popular attraction for visitors and tourists. Some 2,000 visitors a month came during summer vacation. They only bothered Bill when they didn't respect that this was a working light station.

"And some of the screwballs—I'm telling you," an exasperated Bill said decades later. "We opened at two o'clock, but they'd come in there a half-hour early, sit there and eat their lunch, and throw papers out the window right in front of our house or in front of the fog signal. Banana peels, orange peels—right out. I'd go down, make them get out, and clean it up."

People often came through the gate outside of visiting hours and headed to the light. That lit Bill's fuse.

"I'd tell 'em to turn around and leave. And they'd gripe, 'I'm a taxpayer and I have a right to come in here.' I'd go over to the side of the building and pull off a little piece of paint that was peeling away and give it to 'em. 'Here. That's for your taxes.'"

Most visitors were a pleasure; Bill especially enjoyed having school children come out. Field trips from school classes in Mendocino and Fort Bragg were common. "We'd have a whole busload of kids. I'd take 'em down to the light tower and walk 'em through."

"Once in a while, something would be missing. But it wasn't vandalism, it was just school kids. We had stop watches hanging around to check the light and fog-signal. Sometimes, one of those would disappear. Didn't mean much. All I had to do was order another one."

In January 1960, a series of storms, originating off the Gulf of Alaska, began lashing the California Coast. But nothing over the previous seventy-five years matched what hit the central and northern coasts a month later, beginning February 8.

At Monterey Bay, the surf catapulted huge boulders onto roads, ripping apart the asphalt and forcing closures. In Santa Cruz, waves swept over the municipal pier. In the Sierra Nevada Mountains, the Winter Olympic Games were threatened as heavy rains saturated Squaw Valley. (Only when the rain turned to snow in the late afternoon, dropping eighteen inches of powder, did Olympic officials breath a sign of relief.)

Off the Golden Gate Bridge, the 529-foot wine-tanker *Angelo Petri* was disabled by mountainous ocean swells that broke over her deck as she rolled and pitched in the storm. The ship's third engineer was in the engine room, far below deck.

"The sea came down the stack and ventilators," he told a reporter from the *Santa Cruz Sentinel*. "Water doused the main switchboard and that was that. It shorted out everything."

The incapacitated ship drifted nearly six miles before her anchors caught on a sandbar west of Fleishhacker Pool near the San Francisco Zoo. The Coast Guard, along with three tugboats, made a remarkable rescue, somehow managing to attach heavy towlines to the lunging *Angelo Petri* and pull her through the Golden Gate and into San Francisco Bay where she was later repaired.

Meanwhile, the Redwood Empire—including Point Cabrillo—was being bludgeoned with a combination of gale-force winds, heavy rains, and thunderous waves. The storm hit the Mendocino Coast at 9 A.M. Extreme surf and flooding closed Highway 1 and rising waters at Big River kept it closed throughout the next day. The bridge at Doyle Creek was closed when floodwaters swept over the roadway and clogged it with logs and debris. Winds of fifty to sixty miles per hour tore electrical power lines from their poles. In some areas, over twenty inches of rain fell during the three-day period. Just south in Point Arena, large sections were torn from the pier at Arena Cove. Dead fish and abalone, pounded and torn off rocks, lay scattered along the shore.

As officer-in-charge, Bill had received storm warnings from the Coast Guard, but no one could have known its ferocity. "We started the light up in the morning," said Bill. "I thought we might not be able to reach the tower later, so we kept it going the whole time."

Seas grew larger and more violent as the day progressed. Monstrous waves—as high as four-story buildings—slammed into the cliffs. Water surged over the bluffs and far past the fog-signal building and light, which stood forty feet above sea level.

"One of these [waves]," the *Mendocino Beacon* reported, "caught the keeper's delivery truck as it stood just east of the building and raised it clear off the ground. Before the seas had abated, they tore away some thirty to forty feet of surface soil back from the ocean bluff."

Bill said the wave surge extended one hundred yards past the light tower. At 9 P.M., the Coast Guardsman on-watch set out to check the engines and equipment. With the gale and rain pounding against him, he struggled to reach the tower. When he returned, he pounded on the head keeper's front door, a mix of rain and seawater drenching him as he waited.

"Water's coming through the fog-signal down there!" he yelled. "The

The aerial photo was taken from a Coast Guard plane the day following the February 1960 storm. At its height, the storm's white-water surged repeatedly 100 yards beyond the light tower. The heavy rear door behind the building is missing in this picture. (Courtesy of Point Cabrillo Light Keepers Association)

back of the building's torn out!"

Bill ordered everyone to their houses. There was nothing anyone could do but watch, wait, and hope. Through the wind-whipped rain, Bill cautiously ventured toward the light to inspect the conditions. Looking seaward, he could see the revolving light beam sweep across the crest of waves before the mammoth swells exploded on the cliff's face. Great sheets of water slammed the building.

Bill retreated to the house and called the District Office. "There will be no foghorn tonight." The broadcast went out to ships every five-minutes: "Steer clear of Point Cabrillo."

With each wave-strike, a seething mass of water quickly swept inland. Only the slope of the headland slowed its momentum. Overnight, waves broke through the wooden rear of the lighthouse, tearing off the heavy back door and shattering siding like pipestems. The *Press Democrat* in Santa Rosa reported, "Concrete sidewalks about the lighthouse were uprooted. Fifty-pound concrete covers—for the underground gasoline storage—were picked up and tossed like chips hundreds of feet from

Storm damage at the fog-signal building included the large generator shoved from the back of the building to the front. It had been bolted to the floor. (Courtesy of Point Cabrillo Light Keepers Association)

the tanks."

During the night, Isabel heard a rumbling sound like that of a stampede of horses. What could produce such a thunderous pounding? She had no idea.

"I couldn't wait for the next morning to get out and see what it was," she said.

At daylight she saw what she'd heard: the waves had hurled boulders inland, in some cases more than 100 feet beyond the bluffs. "Those rocks weighed hundreds of pounds," Bill said. "We had to get a bulldozer in to shove 'em back in the ocean."

The lower floor of the light was home to a large Caterpillar generator/compressor, which was bolted to the floor at the rear of the room. When Bill examined the equipment the next morning, he found the machinery had been ripped out of its bolts and shoved to the front.

A foot of mud and sand layered the floor. It would take weeks for the engines and generator to be repaired. Carpenters came up from Yerba Buena Island to fix damage to the building and sections of sidewalk that had been destroyed.

The storm ruined everything on the lower floor of the fog-signal. Repairs eventually cost $30,000, ten times that in today's currency.

Damage was extensive across the entire area. Fishing boats had been wrecked in Noyo Harbor. The massive stone jetty had taken a beating. Army Corps of Engineers estimated that the storm caused $50,000 damage to Noyo Harbor's North Jetty. Huge stones had been dislodged from the side-slopes and from under the concrete cap where forty feet of cap was now completely undermined.

"There was an old fella from Mendocino; he was ninety-something years old," Bill recalled. "He came down to the station and told me, 'I never saw anything like this.'"

In the early 1960s, word began to spread about something that struck fear in the soul of every light-keeper worth his salt: Automation.

"You could see it coming," Owens said. "There was a lot of talk, rumors going around."

Technological advancements had slowly evolved. Lighthouses had been surpassed in efficiency by radio beacons, which were then surpassed by marine radar, electronic charts, and eventually, the Global Positioning System. The minute new technology was installed—and it became cheaper to run without a light keeper—automation began to gradually sweep across the light stations of America.

The era of the lighthouse keeper was drawing to a close. Owens knew it—and didn't like it. "Anything automatic goes haywire just when you need it," he said in a National Geographic publication. "Flesh and blood can do something in an emergency. What can a bell buoy do? You can't even hear it in a bad storm."

It had been a career he loved. A career of service that he'd been proud to be part of. But it was about to end.

By fall 1962, a new commander had been assigned to oversee light stations in Bill's group. From the beginning, there were personality clashes between the two. And Bill, now a thirty-two-year veteran of lighthouses, had had enough. He would turn sixty-two in December.

Retirement Day, February 28, 1963. Commander Capinah of the Fort Point Group stands with Isabel, Bill, and a civilian dignitary before the ceremony. (Courtesy of Point Cabrillo Light Keepers Association)

He didn't have to tolerate the Coast Guard attitude toward civil service keepers or their nonsense any longer. It was clear to Bill that his already-flickering patience had now been extinguished.

The admiral had asked him to stay on. "You can stay seven more years if you want."

But things had changed in the 12th District. And Owens was now under the authority of the new commander. Bill had trouble with him from the start.

The officer came to Cabrillo one day, and it wasn't long before sparks flew.

"He didn't know a thing about lighthouses, and he was gettin' my goat!"

"I'm putting in for my retirement," Bill told the new commander.

"How soon do you *want* it?'"

"Just as quick as I can get it."

Within the week, Owens submitted his letter of resignation. He was going out, but on his own terms. Bill continued work until the arrival of a new officer-in-charge could be arranged. From that time on, Point

Cabrillo would be run not by a United States Lighthouse Service keeper, but by Coast Guard men.

Bill's final day of work was February 28, 1963. The retirement ceremony took place aside the light tower on a sunny Thursday morning. Gathered for the event were enlisted men from the Point Arena and Point Cabrillo light stations. Local dignitaries, friends and family filled the chairs. The Coast Guard wisely asked a different officer, the Fort Point Group Commander, to officiate the event.

Owens wore his United States Lighthouse Service uniform, smartly topped by his white cap with the wreath and lighthouse emblem. Commander Capinah's speech cited accomplishments from Bill's distinguished career and presented Owens with letters of commendation and his retirement papers.

Bill Owens accepting the Albert Gallatin Award at his retirement ceremony. The event was held aside the light tower at Point Cabrillo. (Courtesy of Point Cabrillo Light Keepers Association)

Finally, by order of the Secretary of the Treasury, the light keeper was presented with the Albert Gallatin Award—the highest honorary career service award given to a federal employee.

After the ceremony, Bill and Isabel returned to the middle house and quietly celebrated with friends. Talk centered on the future.

Later that night,

The third-order Fresnel lens at Point Cabrillo. (Author photo)

after everyone had left, Bill and Isabel finished packing and sipped cups of coffee in their dining room. It was a lovely wood-paneled setting with a fireplace at one end. Here, the two had shared a thousand meals together.

They spoke of the day they left for Conception 32 years earlier. The girls. Point Sur. Shipwrecks. The war. Point Arena. The challenges they had faced together—and overcome.

Isabel reached across the corner of the table, covered her husband's hand with her own, and said, "You did a good job, Bill."

He didn't smile easily, but a hint of one touched his face. He knew he had.

The last civilian lighthouse keeper on the West Coast, and one of the last in the nation, was content. Owens had completed his course—honorably performing his duties for thirty-two-years—at four California light stations.

The following morning, packed and ready, Bill and Isabel walked through the front gate and across the gravel to their car. Pausing, they turned to gaze at the light station and the tower in the distance. Bill drove the car slowly away. Then, as he had so often done before, he opened the gate, drove through, and closed it behind him.

Chapter Sixteen

Postage Due

For the first time in thirty-two years, Bill and Isabel Owens made their home away from a light station. The *Mendocino Beacon* announced the news with a small front-page headline, "Owens retires from Coast Guard."

Knowing that Bill's retirement was nearing, the couple had bought a home in Mendocino a few years before, "but it needed a lot of work," Isabel recalled. In a fortunate turn of events, someone offered to buy the house—for twice the amount the Owenses had paid for it. They happily agreed to the sale and, near the end of 1962, bought a new home on Airport Road in Little River, just a few miles south of Mendocino. During free moments in their last months at Cabrillo, they had prepped their new home for occupancy—furnishing rooms with tables, chairs, and beds—including one for Pug.

By the day they left the light station, all was ready. Bill and Isabel moved into their new place and eased into retirement.

On major holidays, the Owens family gathered in Little River. Not surprisingly, the grandkids missed the adventurous setting of the light station.

"When our children were young," wrote Joan, "the only place they wanted to spend Thanksgiving and Christmas at was Grandma and Grandpa's at the lighthouse. They loved listening to Grandpa tell stories of his experiences. And he enjoyed telling them."

In the years after Bill retired, when the Coast Guard had trouble with the light at Point Arena, they would occasionally call him. The calls for help infused him with a subtle sense of pride; *sometimes, the old guys know more than the new guys.* On those occasions, the inspector would send a government car up for Bill. He'd go to the station and show them how to fix the problem—as he did one day when the first-order lens stopped turning.

"That lens runs in a mercury bath," he explained decades later. "The whole thing sits in like a barrel. And the barrel has got mercury in it. And the lens and bath are so precision-made that nobody knew how to get in there anymore when it stopped."

Bill peered inside. "It's the mercury," he told the Coast Guard officers. "You've only got a quarter of an inch space between that big foot and the sides. The lens turns round and round and, over time, that mercury grinds up just like dust. You've got to pull the top and take a couple of tongue depressors and flip the dust out."

He had it fixed in no time.

On another occasion, a Commander Olsen was on hand when Bill was called in. As the veteran keeper assessed the mechanism and explained the fix to everyone in the lantern room, the commander shook his head.

"Oh, it can't be," he said.

"It *is*," said Bill.

"Nah. It can't be."

Bill wasn't on the payroll and had nothing to lose in speaking his mind—not that he'd been shy about doing so even when he *was* on the payroll.

"Well, if you knew so damn much about it, what the hell did you have me come all the way down here for?'"

Owens put on his cap, headed down the steps, jumped in the car, and drove home, fuming.

Later, he learned from another officer on hand that when Olsen left the lantern room, two machinists who had listened to Bill's instructions got the lens rotating—by following every step of his advice. It was a satisfying report to hear, and one that left a small smile on his face.

The encounter was emblematic of the occupation. Light keepers were rarely given the credit they were due. The profession went underappreciated—until something malfunctioned. And even then, the seasoned keeper's insights might be ignored.

Their work was performed around-the-clock—and in all kinds of weather. Light beacons were kept shining and foghorns bellowing. The keeper—like a skilled umpire in baseball—went unnoticed until he made a rare mistake. Ship officers may have appreciated them while at sea. But, just as likely, those same officers would not give the light and horn a second thought once they'd safely reached port. "Thank yous" were unheard of.

America's original lighthouse was built at Boston Harbor in 1716, sixty years before the Declaration of Independence was written. For the next 223 years, the beacons of the Lighthouse Service, and its predecessors, were the centerpieces of navigational aids to ships at sea. In California, after 1850,

Bill and Isabel's final formal photo. (Courtesy of Owens Family)

lighthouses had guided everything from four-masted sailing ships to massive modern freighters and liners.

But the days of the lights were now numbered.

As it happened, the Coast Guard would be the service branch that, with Roosevelt's Reorganization Act, closed the United States Lighthouse Service down. Eventually, technology would have done the same. The wave of automation that began in the late 1960s had reached every lighthouse in the country by April 1998. Appropriately, America's first lighthouse, Boston Harbor, was the last to be automated.

Bill's life as a keeper was twined with an array of themes, one of which was him continually proving himself worthy amid a Lighthouse Service that had initially refused to hire him—and his battles with a Coast Guard system that tried to force him out.

He proved them all wrong.

Among the letters received by Owens upon retirement was one from Admiral E.J. Rowland. President Kennedy had appointed Rowland in 1962 as Commandant of the Coast Guard.

February 28, 1963

Dear Mr. Owens,

My attention had been called to the fact that you will retire from the position of keeper in the 12th Coast Guard District at the close of 28 February 1963, after having rendered more than 32 years of honorable service, principally in the former Lighthouse Service and in the Coast Guard. I take pleasure in congratulating you on your long and efficient service and entertain the hope that you may enjoy the leisure afforded by relief from active duty.

Sincerely Yours,

E.J. Rowland
Admiral, United States Coast Guard

"The admiral's a nice fellow," Bill said with his wry smile. "But it's funny. He sent the letter out to me, and it had 'Postage Due' on it. I'm gonna save that envelop and if he ever comes out this way, I'm gonna show it to him."

Epilogue

I n France, Augustin Fresnel continued to develop new concepts in optics following the introduction of his unsurpassed lens. But his health, which had been poor throughout his life, deteriorated in the winter of 1822 with a persistent cough he could not shake. He was soon diagnosed with tuberculosis. He died in 1827 on Bastille Day. He was only thirty-nine.

The technology Fresnel developed would still be in use two-hundred years later in the fields of photography, imaging, magnification, illumination, projection, and solar power—even in virtual-gaming headsets. Today, at least seventy-five Fresnel lenses continue to operate from lighthouses on the coasts, lakes, and bays of the United States alone.

The 18th District superintendent Harry Rhodes, who initially declined to hire Bill, lived out his retirement years in Berkeley with his wife, Harriet. Rhodes died in 1947 at the age of seventy-six.

After Bill's retirement in 1963, his love for fishing was untethered.

He and Isabel frequently carried their gear to fish for salmon at nearby Big River, which empties into Mendocino Bay. It took a stroke, eventually, to keep Bill from casting his line. That happened in the mid-1970s. Although he recovered reasonably well, he lost strength in one of his legs and walked with a cane thereafter.

In 1982, my wife Caren and I spent three days interviewing Bill, then eighty-one, and Isabel, age seventy-eight, at their home in Little River.

At the conclusion of our second day—a time of stories and laughter—Caren and I prepared to return to our B&B. From his chair, Bill removed his pipe, pointed his index finger at us, and said, "You know what I'm gonna do to you? I'm gonna take you all out to dinner!" The invitation took us by surprise. We treated the offer as a too-kind-to-accept gesture and politely declined.

The official seal of the U.S. Light House Service that Bill served for thirty-two years.

"Please don't say no," said Isabel. "I haven't been out to dinner for two years."

Bill made a reservation for us at Fort Bragg's Piedmont Inn, a place he declared was "the best restaurant around."

The evening evolved into one Caren and I would never forget. Bill and Isabel were delightful company throughout. Later, they drove us by Point Cabrillo, where their family had been stationed so many years before.

The car rolled to a stop just outside the locked entry gate.

"Our house was just beyond those Cypress trees," said Isabel softly, a long-distance gaze in her eyes.

Decades later, I told the "dinner story" to the Owens youngest daughter, Diana. Now in her eighties, she laughed and said, "Dad must have liked you. He never took anybody out to dinner!"

By early 1984, Bill Owens, now eighty-three, was in declining health. At the end of April, Isabel took him to the hospital where he suffered another stroke—far more devastating than the first. He died on May 3, 1984.

"I was with him at the last," Isabel wrote in a letter. "I'm not sure he knew I was there, but I hope so."

In the years to come, Isabel devoted much of her time to documenting their lighthouse experiences. She had saved and organized every letter Bill had received from the Lighthouse Service. Eventually, she convinced her six daughters to write down their childhood memories. Together, their notes created a "logbook" of family life at the light stations that have proved a valuable aid to researchers, myself perhaps foremost among them.

In 1985, she made a visit to the Point Sur Light Station. Shirley and Sarah arranged it through a California State Parks Ranger. They kindly invited me to accompany them. It was Isabel's first time on the station in nearly fifty years.

The ranger opened the padlock on the door of the middle triplex dwelling—the section the Owens family occupied when Bill became second assistant. The room was dark, its windows having been boarded-up years before. Splotches of water dotted the concrete floor and plaster peeled from walls. Beams from our flashlights cut through the cold and musty darkness.

Isabel seemed to be standing in two places at once. Or, in two eras—as if it were 1937 for her. She released the handles of her walker. In the dim light, she stood with both hands held in front of her—as if warming them by a fire. Then, she slowly moved them side-to-side, and said, "The kitchen was in the far corner. The dining room table was here. The stairway is down at the end of the room now, but it wasn't then. It went from just inside the door up along this wall."

Isabel and I stood beside each other, separated by five feet—and five decades.

She eventually sold the house in Little River and moved into an assisted living unit in Willits, thirty-six miles east of Mendocino. Her love and appreciation for Bill never wavered. She remained proud of him for his grit, persistence, and devotion to duty.

Isabel died in 1995 at the age of ninety-one.

In the years that followed, the fates of the four light stations where Bill Owens served varied widely.

The once-proud Point Conception Light Station was automated in 1973. Nearly all its buildings have been demolished. Only the light tower and first assistant dwelling on the east side of the hilltop remain—both in a serious state of disrepair. In 2013, the first-order Fresnel lens was removed and placed at the Santa Barbara Maritime Museum. Excellent lighthouse exhibits now surround the lens that is prominently displayed there.

The light station at Point Sur is now a California State Park. A volunteer group, Central Coast Lighthouse Keepers, has for several decades participated in extensive and ongoing restoration of the light station. Public tours are available, and the already-impressive condition of the station is ever-improving.

At Point Arena, in 1984, the non-profit organization Point Arena Lighthouse Keepers leased the lighthouse property. The group became the official owner of the property in 2000, "due to the diligent historic preservation and education efforts of the organization." The old cottages of the Owens era were razed by the Coast Guard long ago. But the PALK has remodeled the remaining Coast Guard dwellings and visitors can now enjoy overnight stays at the station—as well as visit the museum in the original fog-signal building and climb the light tower.

Nine years after Bill Owens retired, the light at Point Cabrillo was automated and personnel removed. The Point Cabrillo Light Keeper Association now operates the station in cooperation with California State Parks and Coast Guard. The association's goal is to return the light station to its original state. The third-order Fresnel lens that sits atop the tower, like the enchanting station itself, is a spectacular sight to see.

Major restoration work began on the Cabrillo light station in 1996. The middle house, where the Owens family lived, was renovated in 2006. When the dining room's wood paneling was carefully removed, the restoration team discovered an old tobacco tin hidden between the wall studs.

Though Bill was a pipe smoker, the tin clearly pre-dated him. Men of the original 1909 construction crew had carefully placed it there as a time capsule of sorts—correctly figuring someday in the future someone would discover what they had left.

The tin was a Union Leader box of Cut Plug—about the size of a small toaster. Inside the box was a piece of old-growth Douglas Fir—signed in pencil by two Scotsmen who had been part of the original construction crew. As the 2006 restoration was completed, the box was replaced in the same wall location, behind the original paneling, with the signatures of the current team added.

Of the six Owens daughters, three have died. Joan was the first to pass at age seventy-five, followed by Sarah, who lived to be eighty-five. Shirley, the oldest, died at ninety-three.

But three Owens girls still abide. Dixie Spence is ninety-two and lives in Federal Way, Washington. Jean Carpenter is eighty-nine and lives in Loveland, Colorado. Diana Brown, the youngest of the six, is now eighty-four and resides in Eureka, California. Dixie, Jean, and Diana each have adult children living close by.

Together, the girls and their husbands enriched Bill and Isabel with eighteen grandchildren and twenty-six great grandchildren—at last count.

After Bill passed away, Isabel told me, "He often said he wanted to be cremated with no special services. I won't say what he had suggested we do with his ashes."

Isabel honored his request. The family held a small, quiet service. Bill's ashes were buried next to their infant daughter, Susan, at the Odd Fellows Cemetery a few miles north of Point Arena, beyond which the sea still churns with untold stories of those who quietly protected sailors now gone.

Acknowledgments

It is to the entire Owens family that I wish first to express my heartfelt gratitude. To Bill and Isabel for investing time in me as a young man who was simply interested in their story. To Shirley and Sarah, who long ago shared recollections with me—and invited me to join them, along with Isabel, in a pilgrimage to Point Sur fifty years after the family had been stationed there.

I am indebted to Dixie and Jean for joyfully engaging in interviews with me. To Joan, whose written memories of her life on a light station enhanced this book. And finally, to Diana and Joe Brown I am particularly grateful.

Diana became a workhorse for me, sharing extensive family documents, photographs, and pursuing answers to questions I asked. When I found myself needing clarification of a story, Diana either provided the missing piece or called Jean or Dixie find it. Every visit, interview, and phone call with the Browns was a pleasure for me.

Others contributed significantly to this project. My thanks extend also to:

Jen Lewis of the Point Cabrillo Light Keepers Association. Jen met twice with Caren and me at the light station. She graciously shared photos from the organization's archives, walked us through the Owens home on the station, and took us into the light tower. Her disposition brightened an otherwise rainy and windy day for us.

Michael Semas kindly granted me permission to use a photograph from his historical collection. He possessed the best photo I'd seen of the light station and wreck of the Pacific Enterprise at Point Arena.

Teri Bushgen of Mendocino assisted in our access to the Owens dwelling at Point Cabrillo—trusting us and the merit of the project. I will always remember her refreshing willingness to help.

Michael McDowell, retired educator and geologist, provided valued insight regarding the geological features of Point Conception and aided in their description.

Carol O'Neil from the Central Coast Light Keepers Association shared past editions of their lighthouse quarterly with me. The information and photos were helpful in conveying the history and atmosphere of Point Sur.

Robert Sanchez, Becky Baker, and Cathy Turley each spent extensive hours reviewing *The Last Lighthouse Keeper*. Their "fresh eyes" spotted errors I had missed—though if any remain, and I suppose there are a few, I'm responsible! Each of the three offered valued feedback on the text, its organization, and the stories contained therein. I am grateful for their practical support and encouragement in the process.

Docents at Point Sur, Point Arena, and Point Cabrillo went out of their way to assist me in accessing information and on-site locations that aided enormously in my ability to describe the events that occurred at each station.

And most helpful of all, most encouraging, supportive, inspiring, and deserving of my wholehearted gratitude, is my wife, Caren. It was Caren who, over forty years, never forgot the importance of Bill and Isabel's story. It was Caren who, when asked if I should take on the Owens story—a project which would take well over a year to complete—told me it was the right thing to do.

References

Miscellaneous information regarding individuals was obtained through hundreds of documents, including lighthouse records, lighthouse visitor logs, birth and death certificates, government appointment records, military records, newspaper articles, census records, voter registrations, and more available through on-line search sources. Direct interviews produced much of the material for the personal stories. Specific sources for some of the book's more prominent topics are:

Augustin Fresnel and Lens

America's Lighthouses, Francis Ross Holland, Jr. 1972.

Fresnel—Genius of Illumination, Sea Frontiers, Carol Vanderwoude, November-December 1981.

The Fresnel Lens, Thomas Tag, USLHS.org.

Fresnel Lens Orders, Sizes, Weights, Qualities and Costs. United States Lighthouse Society, uslhs.org.

Molecular Expressions, Pioneers in Optics, micro.magnet.fsu.edu.

Scientist of the Day/Augustin-Jean Fresnel, Dr. William Ashworth, Linda Hall Library, University of Missouri-Kansas City.

The Rise of the Wave Theory of Light: Optical Theory and Experiment in the Early Nineteenth Century, Jed Buchwald. Archive.org.

Balloon Bomb

In 1945, a Japanese Balloon Boom Killed Six Americans, Five of them Children, in Oregon, Francine Uenuma, *Smithsonian*, May 22, 2019.
Minister Tells of Blast, *The Bend Bulletin*, June 1, 194.
The Survivor, Malcolm Epley, *Vancouver News-Herald,* June 1, 1945.

Beach Patrols

Beach Patrol, United States Coast Guard, coastguardmodeling.com.
German Sabotage and Espionage in the United States Curing WWII, History Collection.com.
How Pearl Harbor Attack Changed Oregon Coast, Washington Coast: Beach Patrols. Beachconnection.net.
Humboldt County's Participation in World War II, C Andrew McGuffin, April 1996, scholarsowrks.calstate.edu.
The Beach Patrol and Corsair Fleet, Dennis Noble, media.defense.gov.
The Beach Pounders, Malcolm Willoughby, August 1957, U.S. Naval Institute, usni.org.
The Mounted Beach Patrol, Roger Durham, Army Heritage Museum, 2009, army.mil.
WWII Beach Patrol Memorialized, Jessie Faulkner, July 30, 2018, Times-Standard.com.

Bill and Isabel Owens

Bill Owens, Officer in Charge, Transferred, *Mendocino Beacon*, March 31, 1945.
Change In Lighthouse Keepers, *Mendocino Beacon*, February 14, 1948.
Description of Cabrillo coast, *Oakland Tribune*, December 16, 1956
Interviews conducted by the author, August 2-4, 1982.
Owens Rescue, *Press Democrat* (Santa Rosa), January 4, 1954.
Pajama Party at Lighthouse, *Mendocino Beacon,* March 1, 1947.
United States Lighthouse Service documents, Owens Family Collection.
Written correspondence from Isabel Owens to the author, 1982-1993.
Written records of Shirley Stormes, Sarah Schwartz, Dixie Spence, Joan Silva, Jean Carpenter, and Diana Brown.

Bill Owens Retirement

Life At Little River and Coast Items, *Mendocino Beacon*, March 22, 1963.
Owens family records.

Captain Cogle

Big British Ship Slowly Breaking Up, *Mendocino Beacon*, September 17, 1949

British Ship On Rocks Off California, *London Daily Telegraph*, September 10, 1949.
Half-Century at Sea Draws to End, *Vancouver News-Herald*, August 30, 1949
Home-Bound From Vancouver, Skipper Puts His Ship On Rocks, *Vancouver Daily Province,* September 10, 1949.
Officer Returns From Wrecked Enterprise, *Vancouver Sun,* September 16, 1949
Pacific Enterprise 'Tortured' by Seas, *Vancouver Sun,* September 12, 1949.
Photo of Captain Cogle, *Vancouver Daily Province*, August 26, 1949.
UK Ship Aground On Calif. Rocks, *Vancouver News-Herald,* September 10, 1949.

Chehalis

Craig Yards Will Repair Chehalis, *Long Beach Sun,* June 29, 1933.
Graveyard of Pacific Grips Two More Victims, *Los Angeles Times*, May 30, 1933.
Schooner Chehalis Beached After Collision, *Long Beach Sun*, May 29, 1933.
Third Victim of Fog Docks at Long Beach, *San Pedro News Pilot,* May 29, 1933.

Honda Disaster

Course 095 To Eternity (1980), by Elwyn Overshiner.
Destroyers Hit Rocks in Fog, *Long Beach Press-Telegram,* September 9, 1923.
Findings of Naval Court-Martials Are Approved By Denby. *San Pedro News Pilot*, December 27, 1923.
Honda (Pedernales) Point, California. Naval History and Heritage Command. History.navy.mil.
Hunt Bodies of 19 Entombed in Destroyer Hull, *Los Angeles Record*, September 10, 1923.
Inquiry Court Names Three Ship Officers, *San Bernadino County Sun*, November 1, 1923.
Lieut. Blodgett Is 'Not Guilty,' *Oakland Tribune,* November 10, 1923.
Many Motorists Visit Wrecks, *Los Angeles Times,* September 23, 1923.
Navy wreck probe begins as divers hunt for bodies, *Long Beach Press Telegram,* September 10, 1923.
Warships Going 20 Knots An Hour in Fog, Crash on Honda Rocks, *San Francisco Examiner*, September 9, 1923.
Warships On Rocks, *Los Angeles Evening Post-Record*. September 10, 1923.

Kenkoku Maru

Insight, Kenkoku Maru Shipwreck, Gaye LeBaron, *Press Democrat* (Santa Rosa), Aug. 20, 1978
Kenkoku Maru photo. Sonoma County Library Digital Collection.
Stranded Japanese Ship Reaches Drydock, *Fresno Bee*, May 25, 1951

Lupine Tragedy

Two Lighthouse Tenders Die as Boat Upset, *Oakland Tribune,* November 24,1933.
Two Men Drown Off Point Sur As Boat Upsets, *Pacific Grove Tribune*, November 24, 1933.

Macon

Airship Macon Sinks in Pacific After 81 Rescued By Naval Craft, *San Bernardino County Sun,* February 13, 1935.
Dirigible Exploded Like Paper Bag Says Lighthouse Keeper, *Press Democrat* (Santa Rosa), February 17, 1935.
Lighthouse Keeper Tells How Macon's Top Fin Collapsed, Pomona Progress Bulletin, February 16, 1935.
Macon Inquiry, Pomona Progress Bulletin, February 15, 1935.
Macon Sinks In Sea, *Press Democrat* (Santa Rosa), February 13, 1935.
Tales of Heroism in Macon Crash Told By Survivors, *Ventura County Star,* February 13, 1935.
"The Knave," *Oakland Tribune,* March 1, 1935.
Witnesses on Ship, Shore, tell of Macon Crash, *Modesto Bee*, February 16, 1935.

1906 earthquake

Bay Area Quake: An Ironic Legacy of the 1906 Earthquake, Keith Love, *Los Angeles Times,* October 23, 1989.
Earthquake and Fire Ruin Great City, *Mendocino Beacon,* April 28, 1906.
Earthquake displays at Point Arena Lighthouse Museum.
New Information about the San Andreas Fault. United States Geologic Survey, earthquake.usgs.gov.
The Northern California Earthquake, April 18, 1906. United States Geologic Survey, earthquake.usgs.gov.

1933 Earthquake

The 1933 Long Beach Earthquake, California Department of Conservation, conservation.ca.gov.

Point Arena

Eleven on Blimp Rescued at Sea, *San Bernadino County Sun*, July 15, 1947.
Eleven Saved From Wayward Blimp, *Stockton Evening and Sunday Record,* July 15, 1947.
Grocery Ads, *Press Democrat* (Santa Rosa), August 29, 1944.
Keepers Paint Tower, *Mendocino Beacon*, July 23, 1949.

Nightly Dim Out Of Coast Lights Ordered By Navy, *Fresno Bee*, May 11, 1942.

Pilot Rescued After Dangling 12-Hours From 'Chute in Tree, *Oakland Tribune*, July 19, 1944

Point Arena Crash Kills Six Flyers, *Press Democrat* (Santa Rosa), August 8, 1946.

Point Arena Theater shows, *Mendocino Beacon*, September 12, 1942.

Three Peninsula Flyers Killed In Plane Crash, *Redwood City Tribune*, August 8, 1946.

S.R. Airfield Flyer Killed, *Press Democrat* (Santa Rosa), July 19, 1944

Point Conception

California State Parks Resources Agency, Primary Record, Point Conception Light Station, #42-040392, February 2019.

Harry Weeks, The Keeper's Son. United States Lighthouse Society, Keeper's Log, Winter 2001.

Keepers of the Light, Willard Thompson, 2014, Rincon Publishing.

Pacific Coast Pilot, 1942, Sixth Edition.

Point Cabrillo

History of Cabrillo, *Oakland Tribune*, December 16, 1956.

Lens arrival, *Mendocino Beacon*, October 24, 1958.

Light to Burn is Short Time, *Mendocino Beacon*, May 1, 1909.

Progress at Point Cabrillo Light, *Mendocino Beacon*, September 19, 1908.

Shows Every Indication of Being Able to Awaken the Dead, *Mendocino Beacon*, April 24, 1909.

Site selection, Point Cabrillo for Lighthouse, *Ukiah Republican Press*, February 15, 1907.

Station description, *Press Democrat* (Santa Rosa), April 10, 1955.

Sunday Drive, Description of Light Station, *Press Democrat* (Santa Rosa), April 10, 1955.

The Tuneful Fog Horn is now being tested, *Mendocino Beacon*, April 24, 1909.

Point Cabrillo Storm

Breakers Pound Northern Coast, *Press Democrat* (Santa Rosa), February 9, 1960.

Giant Waves Pound Coast Damaging Lighthouse, *Mendocino Beacon*, February 12, 1960.

Mendocino Battered By Storm, *Press Democrat* (Santa Rosa), Feb, 10 1960.

Tugs Will Try To Free Grounded Wine-Tanker, *Santa Cruz Sentinel*, February 10, 1960.

$250,000 Assured for Noyo Repairs, *Mendocino Beacon*, April 8, 1960.

Point Sur

CCLK Lighthouse Quarterly, Winter 2000-2001.
The Knave Weekday Column, *Oakland Tribune,* June 3, 1936.
The Point Sur Lighthouse, *Fresno Bee,* August 15, 1937

Rumrunning

Bootleggers, Rumrunners, and Blind-Piggers: Prohibition in Ventura County, Andy Ludlum, Museum of Ventura County, Ventura Museum.org.
Grey Ghost, Islapedia.com.
Imported illegality poured in during Prohibition, by Richard Crawford, *San Diego Union Tribune,* August 2, 2008.
Santa Barbara's history in illegal rum running, KCRW.com.
The Rumrunners, sandiegoyesterday.com

Tenders

Sunset, March 1931, Lighthouse Keeping Is Not Light Housekeeping, Mrs. O.R. Berg .

United States Lighthouse Service History

America's Lighthouses, Francis Ross Holland, Jr. 1972.
Chronology of Lighthouse Events, by Thomas Tag, United States Lighthouse Society.org.
History of the Administration of the Lighthouses in America, by Wayne Wheeler, United States Lighthouse Society, uslhs.org.
Lighthouse Inspection Reports Database, by volunteers from the Chesapeake Bay Chapter of the United States Lighthouse Society, uslhs.org.
The Lighthouse Service, 1789-1939, United States Coast Guard, coastguardmodeling.com.

Index

To contact author Stu McDowell:

mcdowellsinpg@yahoo.com

Made in the USA
Las Vegas, NV
14 January 2024

84315411R00144